PRAYER
Part One

INGREDIENTS FOR

SUCCESSFUL INTERCESSION

By Dr. Alan Pateman

BY DR. JENNIFER PATEMAN

AVAILABLE FROM APMI PUBLICATIONS, AMAZON.COM AND OTHER RETAIL OUTLETS

PRAYER
Part One

INGREDIENTS FOR

SUCCESSFUL
INTERCESSION

DR. ALAN PATEMAN

BOOK TITLE:
Prayer, Ingredients for Successful Intercession (Part One)

WRITTEN BY Dr. ALAN PATEMAN
ISBN: 978-1-909132-11-5
eBook ISBN: 978-1-909132-48-1

Published By:
APMI Publications
In Partnership with Truth for the Journey Books **7**
Email: publications@alanpateman.com
www.AlanPatemanMinistries.com

Acknowledgements:
Author/Design/Senior Editor/Publisher: Apostle Dr. Alan Pateman
Editing/Proofreading/Research: Dr. Jennifer Pateman
Computer Administration/Office Manager: Dr. Dorothea Struhlik
Picture reference: "Creation of Adam" by Michelangelo c. 1512

**"O God, bend Us...
I am coming, coming Lord to thee!"**
(Evan Roberts – Welsh Revival)

❖

Dedication

A ministry cannot exist without the practical support and prayers of our partners; you have really helped to make a difference. May God reward all of you, in His unlimited supply of unconditional love and divine favour!

❖

Table of Contents

❖

Introduction

Prayer in itself is a world of discovery! And no one has the full counsel of God on this subject, except Christ Himself! It has been nearly twenty years since I went with the inner impression, to compile information on this vast subject, two separate books on prayer are the result! This one *(part one)* called, **"Prayer, Ingredients for Successful Intercession"** and *part two,* called **"Prayer, Touching the Heart of God."**

I must stress right at the onset that no attempt has been made to exhaust this subject! These books provide more of an *overview* than an exhaustive study, showcasing the vital *ingredients* necessary for all successful praying.

Both are excellent teaching tools, either for the individual or for the local church payer group, that's eager to lay a solid foundation but don't know where to start!

My simplest motive is to encourage prayer as a way of life. Prayer is something that every Christian should have as a dominating factor in their lives, not just a transient life style.

Besides an overview of the important ingredients that are essential in prayer, these two books provide much needed foundational and fundamental basics, which can help anyone, get started on the road of successful praying. Prayer in itself is one of the largest and most important topics of the bible.

Let this book **"Ingredients for Successful Intercession"** teach, challenge and inspire you to go deeper in your relationship with God and to experience the unlimited and life-changing world of prayer.

- Dr. Alan Pateman

❖

CHAPTER 1

The Mystery of Intercession

Intercession is not a ministry gift for the few; in fact each and *every believer* has the calling. It is a lifestyle, something to carry within, so that when the opportunity or need arises we are ready to intercede. We develop this in our individual lives by praying continually.

*I urge, then, **first of all**, that requests, prayers, intercession and thanksgiving be made for everyone, for kings and all those in authority, that we may live peaceful and quiet lives in all godliness and holiness.*

This is good, and pleases God our Saviour, who wants all men to be saved and to come to a knowledge of the truth. For there is one God and one mediator between God and man, the man Christ Jesus.

(1 Timothy 2:1-5)

Notice that there are seven chief reasons (benefits) of a constant prayer life: Peacefulness, Quietness, Godliness, Holiness, Good and pleasing to God, Salvation, and the Knowledge of the truth.

The Interceding Christian

Kenneth E. Hagin in his book, "The Interceding Christian," wrote:

"In the beginning of our study on intercessory prayer, notice the word, *'first'* in 1 Timothy 2:1-4 above. Things work when we follow directions; therefore, we want to take the bible literally and do exactly as it says.

Too many times we say we believe in prayer and let it go at that. You can say you believe in driving an automobile, but that doesn't mean you can drive one. You could learn a lot by studying a handbook on driving, but there are some things you never would learn until you got in an automobile and start driving. **You learn by experience**.

Paul said in the scripture above, 'I exhort therefore, that, first…' **Let's put first things first. We let secondary things predominate, and neglect things that should be first.**

In our spiritual lives we blame God for our failures. We wonder why certain things don't go right, when, really, **we are not putting first things first**. Usually, people are putting themselves first, even when it comes to praying. But the bible doesn't teach that. **Many times prayers are not answered for you because you are putting yourself first.**

Too many times people are like the farmer who prayed, 'Lord, bless me and my wife, my son, John, and his wife – us four and no more.' We may not put it exactly in those words, but that's the extent of our praying much of the time.

Paul said, in 1 Timothy 2:1-4 above, that before we pray for ourselves or our families we should pray 'for kings, and for all that are in authority.' That means we are to pray for our government – for those who are in authority – from the national level down to the local level. A few of us may be doing this now, but not many. If Christians were praying for our leaders, things would not be as they are in our nation" *(Hagin, The Interceding Christian 1-2).*

Therefore intercession is not of selfish-intent and if true intercession is to be successful, it takes a certain level of surrender. As Jesus prayed for Himself in the garden, "…nevertheless, not what I will [not what I desire], but as Your will and desire" (Matthew 26:39 AMP). **This *self-less* requirement on intercessors is precisely why there are so *few* volunteers!**

Still intercession is much more besides (being self-less); it is full of purpose and not something to be approached willy-nilly. It takes certain knowledge of the scriptures for example, to engage with some accuracy. Using The Word is effective means of securing answers to prayer, because it does not return void! It accomplishes. In addition to using the Word to intercede, we must also allow the Spirit to lead *("the sword OF the Spirit"* Ephesians 6:17).

All in all, this means that intercession is not an intellectual activity *(where humanism can creep in),* nor is it for the backslidden and faint hearted! Equally it is not for the elite either – as some try to make it.

Quite simply intercession takes a robust but humble heart! Anyone trying to intercede from pride or self-effort will find it very difficult indeed. That's why intercession remains something that often baffles even the greatest minds! It's not intellect that's needed, but love, the highest ingredient of all – without which even the simplest of Christian activities is void and useless.

What is Intercession?

"Perhaps believers in general have regarded intercession as just some form of rather **intensified** prayer. It is, so long as there is great emphasis on the word **'intensified;'** for there are three things to be seen in an intercessor, which are not necessarily found in ordinary prayer: *identification, agony, and authority*" (Grubb 89).

So what is intercession and are we willing? **Intercession by its very nature is a ministry of unconditional love that stands-in-the-gap** (*usually* for others). This makes intercession and *ordinary* prayer like two different sides of the same coin, essentially the same and essentially different. For instance intercession, as Rees Howells believed, is a higher and deeper realm of prayer, than *ordinary* prayer, and **a lot more intense!**

There is more spiritual involvement; there is more fervency and feeling in the spirit. Our spirit is more involved in intercession than ordinary prayers, and there is a continuous burden until the prayer is answered.

God seeks intercessors *(Isaiah 59:16, Ezekiel 22:30)*. **There is a real mystery as to why God needs our prayers** and why it is the force that breaks the power of evil, releasing God's plan and purpose for His world.

Andrew Murray, in *"The Ministry of Intercession,"* laid a real challenge at our doorstep as individuals and as the church of Jesus Christ.

He wrote:

"There is a world with its needs entirely dependent on and **waiting to be <u>helped</u> by intercession**; there is a God in heaven with His all-sufficient supply for all those needs, **waiting to be asked**; there is a church with its wondrous calling and its surprises, **waiting to be roused** to a sense of its wondrous responsibility and power" (Murray 170).

He Delights in Mercy

There is a God of glory able to meet all our needs. Murray continued, "He delights in mercy, He waits to be gracious, and longs to pour out His blessings. The love that gave the Son to death is the measure of the love that hovers over every human being! And yet it would seem He does not help? If he does so love and long to bless, there must be some inscrutable reason for His holding back."

Scripture says it's because of our unbelief. "It is the faithlessness and consequent unfaithfulness of God's people. He has taken them up into partnership with Himself. **He has honoured them and bound Himself by making their prayers one of the standard measures of the working of His power.**"

Lack of intercession is one of the chief causes of the lack of blessing. Murray concluded, "Oh that we would turn eye and heart from everything else and fix them upon this God who hears prayer, until the magnificence of His promises and His power and His purpose of love overwhelmed us."

The Spirit Intercedes for Us

Meanwhile, the moment we get tired in the waiting, God's Spirit is right alongside helping us along. If we don't know how or what to pray, it doesn't matter. He does our praying in and for us, making prayer out of our wordless sighs, our aching groans.

He knows us far better than we know ourselves, knows our pregnant condition, and keeps us present before God. That's why we can be so sure that every detail in our lives of love for God is worked into something good.

(Romans 8:26 MSG)

The New International Version says, "*…the Spirit himself intercedes for us with groans that words cannot express.*" We also know that Jesus is at the right hand of God interceding for us, at this present moment. Seen clearly in Romans 8:34, **"Christ Jesus, who … is even at the right hand of God and is also interceding for us."**

As His Body we are called to intercede with Him because intercession is a powerful weapon in spiritual warfare. In Isaiah 53:12, it talks of Christ who "*…bore the sin of many, and made intercession for the transgressors.*"

The Hebrew word used for *__intercession__* in Isaiah was *"paga,"* which means: *"to impinge with violence."* Impinge means: *to collide with.* The Vine's Dictionary states that *"paga"* means: *to strike up against, to be violent against, to invade, to come between, to cause to entreat, to meet with, and pray.*

> *And from the days of John the Baptist until now the kingdom of heaven suffereth violence, and the violent take it by force.*
>
> *(Matthew 11:12 KJV)*

The very reason we pray, is not to inform God of what He already knows, but to be used by Him in prayer to help secure a *RELEASE* of His will on earth, just as it is in heaven. Jesus taught this about prayer saying, *"...your will be done on earth as it is in heaven"* (Matthew 6:10).

Basically the Kingdom of God suffers *intercession!* It's the prayerful, or it's the intercessors that truly *apprehend* the Kingdom of God! There is no passivity in prayer. Real prayer is *fervent* because **without prayer there is no *manifestation* of God.**

Facing Satan in Authority

There are two separate aspects of *"paga"* - warfare and travail:

- Firstly, *"paga"* means facing Satan in the name and authority of Jesus Christ on behalf of people, thereby *"striking up against"* and *"colliding with"* him.

21

- Secondly, *"paga"* implies: travail, *"to come between"* or *"to face"* the Father on behalf of people.

Intercession therefore has two main features: **facing Satan and facing God** *(Ephesians 6:10-18).*

Intercession can simply be defined as:

- One who took the place of
- Standing in the Gap

To intercede is to take the place of another, to stand in the gap on their behalf. Jesus' greatest act of intercession was to stand in the gap, by going to the Cross.

> *But he was pierced for our transgressions, he was crushed for our iniquities; the punishment that brought us peace was upon him, and by his wounds we are healed. We all, like sheep, have gone astray, each of us has turned to his own way and the Lord has laid on him the iniquity of us all.*
>
> *(Isaiah 53:5-6)*

It is also our duty to stand in the gap for others in intercession.

> *I looked, but there was no one to help, I was appalled that no one gave support, **so my own arm worked salvation** for me, and my own wrath sustained me.*
>
> *(Isaiah 63:5)*

> *He saw that there was no one, he was appalled that there was no one to **intercede**; so his own arm worked salvation for him, and his own righteousness sustained him.*
>
> *(Isaiah 59:16)*

God is looking for intercessors because the church has not taken its place as priests. Even common people oppress the poor, rob the needy, and deprive foreigners of justice.

> *I looked for someone who might rebuild the wall of righteousness that guards the land.* **I searched for someone to stand in the gap in the wall so I wouldn't have to destroy the land, but I found no one.** *So now I will pour out my fury on them, consuming them with the fire of my anger. I will heap on their heads the full penalty for all their sins. I, the Sovereign LORD, have spoken!*
>
> (Ezekiel 22:29-31 NLT)

Hedge of Protection

People are so bound to destruction; the wrath of God is upon them. God wants people to take up their priestly ministry and *"stand in the gap"* for these people. **"Standing in the gap" involves standing between people and the enemy.** We too can make up the hedge and protect them.

> *He is not a man like me that I might answer him, that we might confront each other in court. If only there were someone to arbitrate between us, to* **lay his hand upon us both**.
>
> (Job 9:32-33)

> *And I cannot defend myself, for you are no mere man as I am. If you were, then we could discuss it fairly, but there is no umpire between us, no middle man,* **no mediator to bring us together.**
>
> (Job 9:32-33 TLB)

As mediators or intercessors we defend people using the Word of God, pleading their case to God. Mediators bring the hand of God and the hand of man together.

God is looking for men and women who will stand in the gap and spend time in an act of intercession. We talk about reaping a harvest; very often we want to be in there reaping, getting involved in the action, but we also need to spend time *"standing in the gap."*

When I minister for God, I can only be fruitful if the prayers of the church have been offered before hand. Only then can true *reaping* be seen during times of ministry. So a **lot rests upon the prayers of all the saints, it's never a one-man show!**

If the church truly understood the power she had been given, when she prayed, she'd never give up so easily! Jesus gave us *(both individually and corporately)*, **"power of attorney,"** in other words **"to act on behalf of another – to stand in the gap"** – through prayer.

The word **"attorney"** in the Concise Oxford Dictionary means: *"**one appointed to act for another** in business or legal matters (power of attorney – **authority to act** thus); **qualified** lawyer, esp. **representing** client in proceedings."*

Prayer is an Active Event

In Joel 2:13 we are told: *"Rend your heart and not your garments."* It also talks about giving birth, *"Yet no sooner is Zion in labour then she gives birth to her children"* (Isaiah 66:8b). This is very profound considering that Zion represents the Church, the Body of Christ.

If we get into labour, which is a state of giving birth in intercession, praying then becomes an active event. Most mothers know that the time of giving birth is a very active and not necessarily pleasant experience. The mother does not even care who hears her scream!

Intercession, travailing in the spirit and giving birth to the things of God, is a noisy activity. Jack Hayford says, **"Just as groans of travail precede birth, so Holy-Spirit-begotten intercessions forecast new life, new hope and new possibilities for individuals trapped in the impossible"** (Hayford 144).

God promises in Joel when we rend our hearts, crying out *(giving birth)*, that afterwards He *"...will pour out my Spirit on all people"* *(Joel 2:28a)*.

Pain is Forgotten

When a woman is giving birth, it is agony. But just as Jesus told it, the moment after the child is born and laid upon the mother's breast, the pain is forgotten and the joy of the new birth overwhelms her! Likewise when interceding, there will be times when we know in the spirit that the breakthrough has happened.

We will know this breakthrough by the experience of joy. We can then rejoice that our prayers have been received and answered in the spirit realm and will begin to see results in the natural realm.

Intercession is a very powerful weapon in the onslaught against the enemy; Satan does not like it. If for example we want to see the Spirit of God move more than He has already, on a housing estate, in relationships, or people who need salvation, then we must be willing to intercede. We need to get into an attitude of wanting to see the will of God released and therefore travailing for them. We will then reap the harvest, which God has prepared.

Paul in Galatians 4:19 said,

My dear children, for I am again in the pains of childbirth until Christ is formed in you.

(Galatians 4:19)

Paul was constantly in a place of weeping before God for his people. **This then must also be the place for us.**

❖

CHAPTER 2

Unconditional Love

Love **[agape]** in the Greek means; *unconditional, pure love. Compassion or tender-hearted [Eusplagchnos] also in the Greek means: Well compassioned, sympathetic, pitiful, tender-hearted.*

*Love never gives up. **Love cares more for others than for self.** Love doesn't want what it doesn't have. Love doesn't strut, doesn't have a swelled head, doesn't force itself on others, isn't always "me first," doesn't fly off the handle, doesn't keep score of the sins of others, doesn't revel when others grovel, takes pleasure in the flowering of truth, puts up with anything, trusts God always, always looks for the best, never looks back, but keeps going to the end.*

(1 Corinthians 13:4-7 MSG)

The above scripture is pretty conclusive; the word used mostly for *"love"* in the New Testament is *"agape."* This is a love that is unselfish and without condition. God has shown us this love by sending His Son Jesus, to die on the cross for us.

> *For God so loved the world that he gave his only begotten Son, that whoever believes in him shall not perish but have eternal life.*
>
> *(John 3:16 KJV)*

We in turn can love God. To love God fully means to lay down our lives and live *completely* for Him (no longer living a self-dominated existence). As God so loves us, we must in turn love others. It is His love, which should be flowing out from us, to the people of this world.

Love Demonstrates the Power of God

"The self must be released from itself to become the agent of the Holy Ghost... Watch Moses, the young intercessor, leaving the palace by free choice to *identify* himself with his slave-brethren" (Grubb 88).

This Love (God's) is not a soppy, mushy kind of love. It is a powerful love, which is direct and forceful at times, demonstrating His power. **God wants us to love in His power,** and not wait for people to come to us, but for us to be reaching out to them with the dynamic love of Christ.

There are millions of people crying out for God, it is our commission and responsibility to reach them. We must say, **"Jesus loves you!"** NOT in a religious way, but in a way that people can see that we mean what we say.

We must give ourselves in love, one to another, meeting each other's needs. **Not a love that demands from others, but a love that is freely given and received, an unconditional love.** We must not be afraid to love *forcefully*; telling and showing people that we love them and that God loves them. This is <u>not</u> a choice, but a command! *(See also Luke 10:25-37 The Good Samaritan).*

> *If anyone boasts, "I love God," and goes right on hating his brother or sister, thinking nothing of it, he is a liar. If he won't love the person he can see, how can he love the God he can't see? <u>The command we have from Christ is blunt: Loving God includes loving people</u>. You've go to love both.*
>
> *(1 John 4:20-21 MSG)*

Strong Love will Confront Sin

If we do not love forcefully, we need to change our attitude and start loving people with more strength. **The world needs the love of God, not a compromising religious kind of love, but a *robust* love.** A strong godly love will confront and expose sin and all that which needs to change.

As the Church of Jesus Christ, we need to operate in bold and godly love and compassion *(particularly characteristic of a prophetic church).*

Jesus moved in an attitude of love and compassion,

> *Jesus had compassion on them and touched their eyes. Immediately they received their sight and followed him.*
> *(Matthew 20:34)*

Paul tells us in Colossians 3:12-15, to clothe ourselves with compassion:

Since you have been chosen by God who has given you this new kind of life, and because of his deep love and concern for you, you should practise tender hearted mercy and kindness to others. Don't worry about making a good impression on them but be ready to suffer quietly and patiently. Be gentle and ready to forgive; never hold grudges.

*Remember, the Lord forgave you, so you must forgive others. **Most of all, <u>let love guide your life</u>, for then the whole church will stay together in perfect harmony.** Let the peace of heart, which comes from Christ; be always present in your hearts and lives, for this is your responsibility and privilege as members of his body. And always be thankful.*

(Colossians 3:12-15 TLB)

Jesus Moved with Compassion

We need to have first and foremost love and compassion for the people whom God is going to bring to us for ministry. I need love and compassion if I am going to break through for God in any area of their lives; I cannot have a judgmental attitude.

The stories people have told me of their sordid pasts, do not shock me anymore, but I must not judge, for all have sinned and fallen short of the Glory of God *(Romans 3:23)*. Jesus walked in divine love and compassion; we need to take on His very nature, the yoke of Christ *(Matthew 11:29)*.

When Jesus saw those that were hurting, the bible tells us He was moved with compassion. *"And when the Lord saw her, He had compassion on her, and said unto her, weep not..."* *(Luke 7:13 NLT)*

Sympathy is <u>NOT</u> Compassion

Perverted love will only sympathise with people, without actively helping them. In fact sympathy has got most of us into the conditions we find ourselves today. With a good pat-on-the-back we've been informed, *"...things will get better,"* but not shown how to get out of our distresses!

Agape love, on the other hand does not come from the soul it comes from God. Only born-again believers can operate in this kind of powerful love. **So *"agape"* is the most powerful and important ingredient for any intercessor.**

> *My command is this: Love each other as I have loved you. Greater love has no one than this that one lay down his life for his friends.*
>
> *(John 15:12-13)*

As intercessors we are to lay down our lives. **Lack of intercession is a lack of love for others**. We must learn to lay down our *(selfish)* lives and to have *"agape"* love. This God-kind-of-love is operated out of an-act-of-the-will and not via fickle feelings. If we wait to feel love for people, we will wait a very long time. In fact it's safe to say that people in general have their very-own-brand-of-weirdness to deal with and loving them doesn't always come easy!

Yet love is the key component for all type of praying. Matthew 5:43-48 tells us that we are to love our enemies and pray for those who persecute us. Paul in Colossians 3:14 tells us when he speaks of clothing ourselves with compassion, kindness, humility, gentleness and patience that over all those virtues, we should put on *love*.

To Love is an Act of the Will

The Apostle John says:

> *My beloved friends, let us continue to love each other since love comes from God. Everyone who loves is born of God and experiences a relationship with God. The person who refuses to love doesn't know the first thing about God, because* **God is love – so you can't know him if you don't love.**
>
> *(1 John 4:7-8 MSG)*

I repeat, that "agape" is the God-kind-of-love and involves an act of our obedience over and above our emotions, (even though emotions do generally follow - but not always!) Those who are born-again, have this God-kind-of-love inside their spirits, via the Holy Spirit "…*the love of God is shed abroad in our hearts by the Holy Ghost which is given unto us*" (Romans 5:5).

> *We can't round up enough containers to hold everything God generously pours into our lives through the Holy Spirit.*
>
> *(Romans 5:5 MSG)*

However it is down to us to "activate" and "initiate" this kind of love. *("Love wasn't put in our hearts to stay, love isn't love till it's given away!")* We can choose to let it loose or to withhold it. Yet this very love is the basis of all Christian activity, revealing different ingredients, with compassion being a prominent feature in prayer, especially intercession.

W.E. Vine's Dictionary explains, God's compassion is:

- to have pity
- a feeling of distress through the ills of others
- to be moved as to one's inwards
- to be moved with compassion
- to yearn with compassion
- to suffer with another
- to be affected similarly
- to have compassion upon
- to be touched with
- to have mercy
- to show kindness
- a heart of compassion

Compassion is NOT sympathy. As previously mentioned, sympathy only soothes and consoles, where true compassion always produces ACTION and moves towards the "solution" not just docile inertness!

The word *"compassion"* in the Greek is *[spagchnizomai]* and it is connected to the Greek word for *guts, bowels and intestines (also used when talking of sacrifice).* It means: *to have our bowels yearn,* **to literally feel something within us compelling us to ACT.**

Compassion is the Father's Heart

Compassion is straight talk. It is not simply a pat on the back, because there is more to love than that. Love will confront us where we are, showing us our sin or error. Then it will show us *how* to walk free in the ways of the Spirit. In other words compassion won't leave us in our mess.

Most people are fed up of hearing about what's wrong with them, what they need to hear is how to get things right! People pay millions of dollars a year all over the world, on self-help and self-improvement programs. Society is possessed with perfecting itself and tormented by its failures.

The Church must NOT employ the condemnation method. Most people are plagued with guilt all their lives and fashion their lives according to it! But, with all the self-help and improvement programmes and all the money involved, one can assume that folk want to clean up and live right and do the best that they can with their lives.

Not everyone wants to live in the gutter or chase false solutions forever. Only the TRUTH made known *(the Good News)* will set them free. That they can get right with God and clean up for good! Their filthy rags can be exchanged for perfect robes of righteousness. **This is true compassion from their heavenly Father.**

Compassion is equal to the Father-heart of God. The reason we do not have God's compassion all too often is that we are thinking of ourselves way too much. Or in other words, we are fixated with ourselves!

To intercede successfully we must have the Father's compassionate heart for people. We need to be able to identify with those we are praying for, as Jesus did.

> *Your attitude should be the kind that was shown us by Jesus Christ, who, though he was God, <u>did not demand and cling to his rights</u> as God, but laid aside his mighty power and glory, taking the disguise of a slave and becoming like men. And he humbled himself even further, going so far as actually to die a criminal's death on a cross.*
>
> *(Philippians 2:6-8 TLB)*

The King James Version of the bible simply says, *"Let this mind be in you, which was also in Christ Jesus" (verse 5)*. But I also like what the Message Bible has to say:

> **Think of yourselves the way Christ Jesus thought of himself.** *He had equal status with God but <u>didn't think so much of himself</u> that he had to cling to the advantages of that status no matter what. Not at all.*
>
> *When the time came, he set aside the privileges of deity and took on the status of a slave, became human! Having become human, he stayed human. It was an incredibly humbling process. He didn't claim special privileges. Instead, <u>he lived a selfless, obedient life and then died a selfless, obedient death</u>…*
>
> *(Philippians 2:5-8 MSG)*

The Person of the Holy Spirit

If Jesus identified with man, so must we, but it's not something we can achieve by our flesh but with the help of the Holy Spirit. We have to be aware of what people are going through whether it's pain, anguish or any other form of brokenness. Only with His help can we exercise true compassion, *"The Spirit of the Lord God is upon me; because the Lord has anointed me... to bind up the broken-hearted..." (Isaiah 61:1 KJV)*

God's love and compassion for the world was demonstrated by the giving of His Son Jesus *(John 3:16).* As we look to Jesus in our lives, we observe the compassion of the Father, for Jesus said, *"He that has seen me has seen the Father" (John 14:9 NKJV).* **Jesus is the will and love of God in action.** In His earthly ministry, He was moved with compassion and compassion aught to move us today!

> *But when he saw the multitudes, he was moved with* ***compassion*** *on them, because they fainted, and were scattered abroad, as sheep having no shepherd.*
> *(Matthew 9:36 KJV)*

> *And Jesus went forth, and saw a great multitude, and was moved with* ***compassion*** *toward them, and he healed their sick.*
> *(Matthew 14:14 KJV)*

> *And Jesus, moved with* ***compassion***, *put forth his hand, and touched him, and saith unto him, I will; be thou clean.*
> *(Mark 1:41 KJV)*

*So Jesus had **compassion** on them, and touched their eyes: and immediately their eyes received sight, and they followed him.*

(Matthew 20:34 KJV)

*When the Lord saw her, he had **compassion** on her, and said unto her, weep not.*

(Luke 7:13 KJV)

*So he got up and went to his father. But while he was still a long way off, his father saw him and was filled with **compassion** for him; he ran to his son, threw his arms around him and kissed him.*

(Luke 15:20)

*It is of the Lord's mercies that we are not consumed, because his **compassions** fail not. They are new every morning: great is thy faithfulness.*

(Lamentations 3:22-23 KJV)

❖

CHAPTER 3

Liquid Prayers

There is another Intercessor, and **in Him we see the** *agony* **of this ministry;** for He, the Holy Spirit, *"maketh intercession for us with groanings which cannot be uttered."* "This One, **the only present Intercessor on the earth,** has no hearts upon which He can lay His burdens, and no bodies through which He can suffer and work, except the hearts and bodies of those who are His dwelling place.

Through them he does His intercessory work on earth, and **they become intercessors by reason of the Intercessor within them"** (Grubb 87).

If we are walking right before God, we will be sensitive to His Spirit. We will feel grief; pain, anguish and sadness come upon us. In response we must ask God, "What is wrong?

What is it you want me to do here, Lord?" Often we will not know this, until we get into prayer.

When the prompting comes, Satan will do his utmost to stop us from interceding, because *it is this level of intercession that causes him the most damage!* How many times have we been prompted to intercede, but have been distracted? We need to be obedient and say, *"Yes Lord, what is it?"* and then begin to intercede.

> *And do not grieve the Holy Spirit of God, with whom you were sealed for the day of redemption.*
>
> *(Ephesians 4:30)*

Not human Sympathy

The Holy Spirit causes us to express weeping so that it brings change in the realm of the spirit. This type of weeping does not originate from the soul realm (human sympathy), but from the spirit realm.

> *A **cry is heard** on the barren heights, the weeping and pleading of the people of Israel, because they have perverted their ways and have forgotten the Lord their God.*
>
> *(Jeremiah 3:21)*

Jeremiah was known as the "weeping prophet." His weeping was intercession on behalf of God's people. He had a desire to see them free from sin and in a relationship with God. **Yielding to the Holy Spirit in weeping is interceding for the sins of the people.**

Oh, that my head were a spring of water and my eyes a fountain of tears! I would weep day and night for the slain of my people.

(Jeremiah 9:1)

There are times when we can be burdened for days; very often we do not know how to handle it. Jeremiah had a burden to see the people set free from sin and have their relationship restored back with God.

This is what the Lord Almighty says: Consider now! **Call for the wailing women to come**; *send for the most skilful of them. Let them come quickly and wail over us till our eyes overflow with tears and water streams from our eyelids.*

(Jeremiah 9:17-18)

There is a call for intercessors, those that are willing to release themselves into wailing for the people. Weeping and wailing helps us to see things from a spiritual perspective.

Now, O women, hear the word of the Lord, open your ears to the words of his mouth. **Teach your daughters how to wail; teach one another a lament.**

(Jeremiah 9:20)

Intercession was needed because death had come. Weeping and wailing expresses our desire to see others saved from spiritual death.

But if you do not listen, I will **weep** *in secret because of your pride; my eyes will weep bitterly overflowing with tears, because the Lord's flock will be taken captive.*

(Jeremiah 13:17)

*Speak this word to them: "Let my eyes overflow with **tears** night and day without ceasing; for my virgin daughter – my people – has suffered a grievous wound, a crushing blow.*

(Jeremiah 14:17)

*My eyes fail from **weeping**, I am in torment within, my heart is poured out on the ground because my people are destroyed, because children and infants faint in the streets of the city.*

(Lamentations 2:11)

*The hearts of the people cry out to the Lord. O wall of the Daughter of Zion, let your tears flow like a river day and night; give yourself no relief, your eyes no rest. Arise, cry out in the night, as the watches of the night begin; **pour out your heart like <u>water</u> in the presence of the Lord.** Lift up your hands to him for the lives of your children, who faint from hunger at the head of every street.*

(Lamentations 2:18-19)

Charles Spurgeon once said that, "...tears are liquid prayers."

God is Raising up a Prophetic People

A characteristic of a prophetic people is that they should live a life of intercession, crying out for His people.

*But if they are true prophets and if the word of the Lord is really spoken by them, let them now make **intercession** to the Lord of hosts, that the vessels which are [still] left* *in the house of the Lord, in the house of the king of Judah, and in Jerusalem may not go to Babylon.*

(Jeremiah 27:18 AMP)

*Wake up, you drunkards, and **weep**! Wail, all you drinkers of wine; wail because of the wine, for it has been snatched from your lips.*

(Joel 1:5)

***Mourn** like a virgin in sackcloth grieving for the husband of her youth.*

(Joel 1:8)

Signs of backsliding are feeling spiritually dry and stale and not wanting to attend church. **Intercession, weeping before God will break this**. Weeping is a sign of repentance for self or other people who are backsliding. This level of intercession is so powerful that it will bring brokenness. We cry out to God, in return He pours out His Spirit and power upon us.

The Holy Spirit is grieved when we turn away; His ministry is to bring us to the throne of God. When we turn away it aborts that which He wants to bring about.

If we are not in a continual state of submission, we will be hard-hearted and insensitive to the Holy Spirit. We need to be in a place before God, ready for when the Holy Spirit calls upon us. **This weeping in the Spirit refreshes, not depresses us!**

Those who sow in tears will reap with songs of joy. He who goes out weeping, carrying seed to sow, will return with songs of joy, carrying sheaves with him.

(*Psalm 126:5-6*)

Weeping Sows Seeds

The weeping is not in vain; it sows seeds in the spirit realm. *"Godly sorrow brings repentance that leads to salvation and leaves no regret, but worldly sorrow brings death"* (*2 Corinthians 7:10*).

> **For godly grief and the pain God is permitted to direct,** *produce a repentance that leads and contributes to salvation and deliverance from evil, and **it never brings regret**; but worldly grief (the hopeless sorrow that is characteristic of the pagan world) is deadly [breeding and ending in death].*
>
> (*AMP*)

If we humble ourselves before God in repentance, He will raise us up. True repentance is feeling godly sorrow, feeling so sorry that we have let God down, that we cry out before Him. Then a determination comes that we never ever want to sin again.

> *I am afraid that when I come again my God will humble me before you, and I will be **grieved** over many who have sinned earlier and have not repented of the impurity, sexual sin and debauchery in which they have indulged.*
>
> (*2 Corinthians 12:21*)

I do admit that I have fears that when I come you'll disappoint me and I'll disappoint you, and in frustration with each other everything will fall to pieces – quarrels, jealousy, flaring tempers, taking sides, angry words, vicious rumour's, swelled heads, and general bedlam.

*I don't look forward to a second humiliation by God among you, compounded by **hot tears** over that crowd that keeps sinning over and over in the same old ways, who refuse to turn away from the pigsty of evil, sexual disorder, and indecency in which they wallow.*
(2 Corinthians 12:20-21 MSG)

We take the place of those who have sinned and have not repented. Jesus is our greatest example, He too wept. *"'Lord, if you had been here, my brother would not have died.' When Jesus saw her weeping, and the Jews who had come along with her also weeping, he was **deeply moved in spirit and troubled**. 'Where have you laid him?' he asked... **Jesus wept**"* *(John 11:32b-35).*

Jesus was not weeping from the natural realm; He was interceding by the Spirit on behalf of Lazarus. If Jesus could weep in front of men, then we too should be willing to weep in intercession.

*During the days of Jesus' life on earth, he offered up **prayers and petitions with loud cries and tears**, to the one who could save him from death, and he was heard because of his reverent submission.*
(Hebrews 5:7)

❖

CHAPTER 4

Groaning Produces Life

Groanings are an expression of the Holy Spirit in prayer, which we yield to as we approach the throne room of grace in prayer.

*In the same way, the Spirit helps us in our weakness. We do not know what we ought to pray, but the **Spirit himself intercedes for us with groans** that words cannot express.*

(Romans 8:26)

To groan is to voice a deep wordless prolonged sound, sometimes expressive of grief. These expressions come up out of our spirit man, from the Holy Spirit within.

*During that long period, the king of Egypt died. **The Israelites groaned** in their slavery and cried out, and their cry for help because of their slavery went up to*

47

God. **God heard their groaning** *and he* **remembered his covenant** *with Abraham, with Isaac and with Jacob.* **So God looked on the Israelites and** <u>was concerned about them.</u>

(Exodus 2:23-25)

Groaning for Deliverance

The children of Israel groaned for deliverance, God heard them and remembered His covenant.

The Lord said, I have indeed seen the misery of my people in Egypt. **I have heard them crying** *out because of their slave drivers, and I am concerned about their suffering.* **So I have come down to rescue them** *from the hand of the Egyptians and to bring them up out of the land into a good and spacious land, a land flowing with milk and honey - the home of the Canaanites, Hittites, Amorites, Perizzites, Hivites and Jebusites.*

(Exodus 3:7-8)

True deliverance comes from an inner yearning for freedom and not from having hands laid on us. There is more to intercession than just tongues; there is a deeper core of prayer. When we are interceding for others or for ourselves, we must begin to groan in the spirit, crying out to God for RELEASE.

In bitterness of soul *Hannah* **wept much** *and prayed to the Lord. And she made a vow, saying, "O Lord Almighty, if you will only* **look upon your servant's misery** *and remember me, and not forget your servant but give her a* *son, then I will give him to the Lord for all the days of his life, and no razor will ever be used on his head."*

*As she kept on praying to the Lord, Eli observed her mouth. Hannah was praying in her heart, and her lips were moving but her voice was not heard. Eli thought she was drunk and said to her, "How long will you keep on getting drunk. Get rid of your wine." "Not so my Lord," Hannah replied, "I am a woman who is **deeply troubled.** I have not been drinking wine or beer; **I was pouring out my soul to the Lord."***

(1 Samuel 1:10-15)

Groaning produces life. When God heard Hannah's groanings, He answered her and she had her child Samuel.

*The Lord looked down from his sanctuary on high, from heaven he viewed the earth, **to hear the groans** of the prisoners and **release** those condemned to death.*

(Psalm 102:19-20)

God heard the groanings of the prisoners and He loosed them form death into life.

Groaning is a High Level of Intercession

As intercessors we can groan on behalf of others and stand in the gap for them. Jesus groaned and interceded on this high level of intercession and so must we.

Jesus knew He was going to raise up Lazarus from the dead, He groaned because of the people's unbelief and in order to **change the spiritual atmosphere.** Jesus was the only one in the Spirit; His was a spiritual reaction to a fleshly environment. Lazarus was dead and **Jesus was interceding for him to be *RELEASED* from death.**

The deaf man only received his hearing *after* Jesus groaned and interceded on his behalf. (Note: in the Greek, "to sigh" also means, "to groan" - see Strong's 4727).

> *After he took him aside away from the crowd Jesus put his fingers into the man's ears. Then he spat and touched the man's tongue. He looked up to heaven and with a **deep sigh** said to him "Ephphatha!" ("Be opened!"). At this, the man's ears were opened, his tongue was loosened and he began to speak plainly.*
>
> *(Mark 7:33-35)*

> *The Pharisees came and began to question Jesus. To test him, they asked him for a sign from heaven. **He sighed deeply** and said. "Why does this generation ask for a miraculous sign? I tell you the truth, no sign will be given to it."*
>
> *(Mark 8:11-12)*

Groaning Breaks Bondage

This was the devil trying to trap Jesus, but He **groaned** and **interceded** and therefore did not fall into the enemy's trap. The devil will also try and tempt us, but as we groan and intercede our weaknesses will also be broken!

Muttering in tongues is not enough; we must practise groaning out-loud. **When we get down on our knees and start groaning, things will change in our lives.** It starts from the depth of our spirit and within a short period of time our whole being is involved. *(That does not automatically mean loud, but does mean fervent!)*

W.E. Vine dictionary explains groans as inward, unexpressed feelings of sorrow. This word is also translated as grief, sigh or murmur.

- Grief   -   signifies pain, of body or mind.
- Sigh   -   suggesting deep drawn.
- Murmur   -   with utterance, to work out with labour.

❖

CHAPTER 5

Travailing Brings Growth

Ll the creation groans and travails in pain. The ultimate consciousness of pain resides in God, because of His perfect love. Through our fellowship with God we are brought into fellowship with the suffering of creation. Our consciousness of the groaning creation is much more acute than if we were outside the Kingdom of God, because we are united to God through Jesus Christ *(see John 15:5).*

The Holy Spirit interprets to us God's consciousness of suffering and makes intercession with groaning that cannot be uttered.

*We know that the whole creation has been **groaning as in the pains of childbirth** right up to the present time Not only so, but we ourselves, who have the first fruits* *of the Spirit, **groan** inwardly as we wait eagerly for our adoption as sons, the redemption of our bodies.*

*In the same way, the Spirit helps us in our weakness. We do not know what we ought to pray, but the Spirit himself intercedes for us with **groans** that words cannot express. And he who searches our hearts knows the mind of the Spirit, because the Spirit intercedes for the saints in accordance with God's will.*

(Romans 8:22-23, 26-27)

God intends for the Church to be His womb on earth, so that His heavenly will can be birthed and manifested. For the will of God to come to maturity, we have to bring it to birth in the spirit realm. It is spiritual labour and just as a woman giving birth, it is a strenuous, spiritual exertion.

Travail is agony and anguish and is a deeper level of intercession than groaning or tongues. It is usually to bring forth revival or renewal in the Church, to bring forth-new life in the Body of Christ.

*Therefore confess your sins to each other and pray for each other so that you may be healed. **The prayer of a righteous man is powerful and effective.***

(James 5:16)

*The prayer of a person living right with God is something **powerful to be reckoned with.***

(MSG)

*The earnest (heartfelt, continued) prayer of a righteous man makes **tremendous power available** [dynamic in its working].*

(AMP)

Elijah prayed earnestly, fervently and powerfully when he was interceding. *"...Elijah climbed to the top of Carmel, bent down to the ground and put his **face between his knees**"* (1 Kings 18:42).

Hearers in the Spirit Realm

We should be hearing what is happening in the spirit. Elijah prayed and sent his servant to see if the rain had begun. Elijah was bringing to birth what he saw in the spirit. We also need to travail and bring to birth those prophecies over our own lives *(see next chapter about bringing to birth).*

We should continue to intercede until the answer comes or else our prayers will be aborted. It is our job to get down on our knees and bring to birth the will of God for our lives and nation. **The answers will come little by little and not as a cascade.**

> ***Before she goes into labour, she gives birth; before the pains come upon her,*** *she delivers a son. Who has ever heard of such a thing? Who has ever seen such things?*
>
> *Can a country be born in a day or a nation be brought forth in a moment? Yet **no sooner is Zion in labour than she gives birth** to her children. Do I bring to the moment of birth and not give delivery? says the Lord.*
>
>
>
> *(Isaiah 66:7-9)*
>
>

Travailing Brings Revival

When the Church starts travailing, there will be a mighty move of revival and many people will be saved. God will bring forth the fruit once we start travailing.

> *My dear children, for whom I am again in the **pains of childbirth** until Christ is formed in you.*
>
> *(Galatians 4:19)*

When people first experience salvation, we must travail for their continual growth and maturity in Christ.

> *Epaphras, who is one of you and a servant of Christ Jesus, sends greetings. **He is always wrestling in prayer for you**, that you may stand firm in all the will of God, mature and fully assured.*
>
> *(Colossians 4:12)*

> *The Lord will march out like a mighty man, **like a warrior** he will stir up his zeal; with a shout he will raise the battle cry and will triumph over his enemies "For a long time I have kept silent, I have been quiet and held myself back but now, **like a woman in child birth, I cry out, I gasp and pant.**"*

> *I will lay waste the mountains and hills and dry up all their vegetation; I will turn rivers into islands and dry up the pools. I will lead the blind by ways they have not known, along unfamiliar paths I will guide them; I will turn the darkness into light before them and make the rough places smooth. These are the things I will do; I will not forsake them.*
>
> *(Isaiah 42:13-16)*

Travail is an Offensive Weapon

Travailing prayers can also be used to attack the enemy; it breaks the hindrances of the devil and brings forth the will of God.

Ask and see: **Can a man bear children? Then why do I see every strong man with his hands on his stomach like a woman in labour, every face turned deathly pale?** *How awful that day will be! None will be like it. It will be a time of trouble for Jacob, but he will be saved out of it.*

In that day, declares the Lord Almighty, **I will break the yoke off their necks and will tear off their bonds; no longer will foreigners enslave them.** *Instead, they will serve the Lord their God and David their king, whom I will raise up for them.*

(Jeremiah 30:6-9)

Travailing Releases the Captives

Men travailed for deliverance from captivity:

Oh, my anguish, my anguish! I writhe in pain. Oh, the agony of my heart! *My heart pounds within me, I cannot keep silent; For I have heard the sound of the trumpet; I have heard the battle cry.*

(Jeremiah 4:19)

Jeremiah was so much in intercession that he was in pain. **We too can stop destruction from coming when we travail.**

At this my body is racked with pain, pangs seize me, like those of a woman in labour. I am staggered by what I hear, I am bewildered by what I see.

(Isaiah 21:3)

He was in pain as a woman in labour because of what he saw in the spirit.

*Lord, they came to you in their distress; when you disciplined them, they could barely whisper a prayer. As a woman with child and about to give birth **writhes and cries out in her pain**, so were we in your presence, O Lord.*

(Isaiah 26:16-17)

The Israelites were in a place of travail as a woman near the time of delivering her child. **It costs to get into deep travail, but there are great rewards.**

❖

CHAPTER 6

Bringing to Birth

The angel Gabriel gave Mary a message *(prophecy)* about bringing forth a ministry *(Christ within her)* that would bless the entire world *(Luke 1:26-38)*. And the natural process that she had to go through to bring Jesus to birth is parallel to the spiritual process that we must go through to bring forth a divinely ordained ministry.

Who hath heard such a thing? who hath seen such things? Shall the earth be made to bring forth in one day? or shall a nation be born at once? for as soon as Zion travailed, she brought forth her children.

(Isaiah 66:8 KJV)

Before there can be a birthing process, we must have a close relationship with God that gives opportunity for the Holy Spirit to plant a seed of faith (a Rhema Word) and vision within us. The vision then grows like a baby in the womb of our spirit. Patience, adjustments, and divine flexibility are required for the long process from conception to birth - delivery.

We can give birth to life or to death. Scripture reveals such:

Sin... when it is full-grown, gives birth to death.
(James 1:15)

...and humbly accept the Word planted in you, which can save you.
(James 1:21)

Don't let anyone steal Your Baby!

Like an expectant mother's womb, our soul is stretched until we feel we can't be stretched anymore! We become as awkward in our spiritual walk (heavy and out of shape), especially in the final trimester, and just as she (a mother) feels after nine long months (after reaching her limit). We too discover that things get much worse before they get better; labour pains prior to delivery are the strongest and most painful!

The 12th hour experience can take a long time and just before a vision, ministry or prophetic promise is brought forth into visible reality, **we go through our darkest hour of labour and stress!**

Like many women in childbirth we begin to think, *"Why did I ask for this, I don't want to go through with this – it's not worth it!"* But if we hold on, flowing and working with the labour pains instead of against them, before we know it, the results of our labour will be full and rewarding. We will have a ministry come forth for all to see.

Like a new baby, that ministry will go through several years where we must take care of it day and night. It will be wholly dependant on us. But as we pour our lives, energy, time and abilities into it, just like we would for a child, with the goal that eventually it will fend for itself, *(be less dependent)* and stand on its own two feet! Once it arrives at this point *(the child/ministry)* will only require our **parental oversight, care, covering and counsel**.

Going through the right Chanel

Those who suddenly become *successful* without going through the proper process will usually not be able to maintain their personal purity or go onto maturity and the fullest possible ministry *(Isaiah 66:7-8)*.

Too many have developed an orphan spirit due to the fact that they were not birthed properly. Paul understood this concept of bringing-to-birth spiritually, when he said, *"My little children, of whom I travail in birth again until Christ be formed in you" (Galatians 4:19)*.

A Young Ministry needs our:

• Life	*(then eventually)*	Parental Oversight
• Energy	"	Care
• Time	"	Covering
• Ability	"	Counsel

Some of us have been discouraged - but we need to see that God is always moving! Below are seven steps that will help us to remain encouraged in the Lord *(1 Samuel 30:6 KJV).*

Seven Steps:

- Find out the will of God – *(vision)*
- Pray in agreement for the fulfilment of that will *(obedience)*
- Refuse any doubt
- Meditate on the promises – *(faith)*
- Give God the praise along the journey *(and don't complain)*
- Do not accept defeat *(discouragement and disappointments)*
- Receiving what you see is always in the now.

The Role of the Midwife

This is a chapter that I am particularly passionate about because all of us at one point or another have needed encouragement to **push-through**. Where most of us discover that, identical to the role of the midwife (who helps to deliver) the Holy Spirit helps us!

When the going gets tough - particularly around the time of delivery - we need to depend heavily on the Holy Spirit to help us bring to birth *(spiritual breakthrough).* We will know instinctively when it's – time. But for any baby to be delivered *(alive),* cooperation with the midwife *(Holy Spirit)* is essential *(pushing and breathing!)*

At this point the life of both mother and child is at risk and a successful delivery is paramount. There is no going back! Figuratively **the delivery symbolises breakthrough and the child symbolises our future and destiny**.

I can share from experience about my own ministry, how important it is to bring a ministry to birth. For me God gave me seeds - seeds of doctorate. Everything I have - He told me beforehand what was going to happen. I followed His direction, the seed was sown and finally that which HE said came to pass.

I allowed His Word to come into my spirit saying, *"Let it be unto me as You have said Lord."* Then I simply refused every other suggestion or seed or opportunity that was NOT of Him, because that would have taken me off course.

We must be this diligent, regardless of how long it takes for the seed of what God has pre-destined for us to step into comes to pass. We must always remember that the Word He gives, takes time to come to fruition.

When we pray we are looking for the seed of divine direction. That's what brings stability – we must stand on the rock of revelation, God's *(Rhema)* Word for us *(Matthew 16:16-18)*. The very rock of revelation of Himself, not an organisation!

We can't Wear somebody else's Revelation

We can serve it, which might be part of our own destiny. Of course each one of us regardless of what seeds are sown and where God's destiny takes us, before anything else we are meant to be a witness. Where we declare the goodness of God, which keeps us proactive within our Christianity. **All of us are called to be part of one Body and the nature of that Body is servant-hood.**

I must emphasise here that when we are born again we become one in Christ, sealed with the Holy Spirit but are still part-empty - seed HAS to be sown – just like the seed of salvation. The bible says that if we accept Jesus Christ as our Lord and Saviour we become born-again *(John 3)*. We become one in Him - sealed with the Holy Spirit.

From that point however, we begin a journey where two things need to happen in order to maintain growth, development and fulfilment in life *(within the Kingdom and reign of Jesus Christ).*

Firstly we need the baptism of the Holy Spirit – to operate in and through us. Secondly - we need the Word (seed) that needs to be sown into our vessel - which we have become now that we are born again. God wants to mould us like clay. Therefore it is impossible to fulfil a Christian life without the revelation that a seed needs to be sown – in order to grow.

Christianity or Existence

Christianity is not an existence where we just worship our Saviour - that to me is just deception. Worship is paramount but if that is all our religion is about then we have missed it. We can lullaby ourselves to sleep and never actually DO what God has commissioned us to do. Even if the songs are anointed, it's still deception, if we never achieve anything beyond that. Obedience moves beyond just worship – which is only *part* of our Christian experience – only *part* of our relationship with God.

God does not just want us to exist, He wants us to fulfil His purposes here on the earth. This is why it's important for each and every one of us to receive the **Rhema Word** of God. Without this, we have no directive for our lives and God certainly did not commission the Church to be aimless and powerless. No! In fact He *empowered* His Body *on-purpose* and *"...according to **His purpose.**"*

> **And we know that in all things God works for the good of those who love him, who have been <u>called</u> <u>according to his purpose.</u>** *For those God foreknew he also predestined to be conformed to the likeness of his Son, that he might be the firstborn among many brothers.*
>
> **And those he predestined, he also called;** *those he called, he also justified; those he justified, he also glorified. What, then, shall we say in response to this?* **If God is for us, who can be against us?**
>
> *(Romans 8:28-31)*

In addition to all of this, let me add that it is vital when speaking of the Rhema Word of God, that we do not automatically think that the Rhema Word that others have received directly from God, is also our Rhema Word.

Although God can speak to us through others, I am speaking more specifically. For example let us not think that because others have revelation, that it is *our* revelation!

When Kenneth Hagin was still alive, many people were quoting him a lot of the time. What they were quoting was his revelation, that he got directly from the Lord – not their own, *(this can develop into deception)*. We need our own revelation from the Lord in addition to what we receive via others. No matter how anointed they were.

Modern day Example

For a more modern day example, many are quoting Joyce Meyer instead today. And as much as I like and admire Joyce, many people are quoting what God said to her and not themselves. This is okay to a point, but **people MUST learn to hear God directly.** I do believe that Joyce Meyer teaches individuals to hear God for themselves, but this will not prevent some people from still quoting her revelation as though it were their own! But that is not Joyce's fault. If people are not quoting Joyce Meyer they are quoting someone else.

Other to this people are preaching a Gospel of information and knowledge *(of human behaviour such as psychology)*, nevertheless it's a **humanistic gospel they are preaching** *(filled with human opinions, reasonings and philosophies)*.

Incidentally humanism is not something that we can escape. It is rife within the Church and the world alike. The more aware we are the better. So for those who are not familiar with this terminology *(humanism)* let me spell it out nice and clearly, using the words of Ulf Ekman in his book, "God the State and the Individual."

Humanism - Man the Measure of Everything?

"Another ideology that has infiltrated the minds of most people today is humanism... the system of thought that denies God's existence and sovereignty and places man at the centre of everything, making all things relative.

Humanism has its roots in the Renaissance period and even prior to that, when the expression 'Man-the measure of everything' was coined... During the Renaissance, the fine arts blossomed and people felt stimulated afresh, as though they had thrown aside the inhibitions that had hindered their creativity. This in itself was not negative...

In short, what happened as a result... was the undermining and disappearance of three foundational biblical principles:

- That God really is an objective reality
- That what He says is objective truth with eternal application
- That He moves and acts in human history

Humanism's starting point is not God, but man. According to humanistic thinking, man is not God's creation; he is just a highly developed animal. The world as a whole does not exist as a result of what God has done. Instead, the world has become what it is today, through spontaneous and random development.

According to humanistic thinking, there is no such thing as a fall into sin. Mankind is simply as it is, and therefore must be permitted to live out its every fantasy, inclination and desire, these being simply 'human.' **As humans, we are not to be burdened with guilt. Man has not fallen from fellowship with God, but is in himself good.**

According to humanistic thought, man is good. There he should not be disciplined or punished, since this is judgmental and hinders his development. Setting limits is restrictive. Man must have freedom to do what he himself deems to be right…

The goal of mankind becomes *self-realization*, and with this reasoning whatever appears to prevent this from happening is labelled as 'sin.' **This is why humanism is generally tolerant toward everything** *except* **the Christian faith.** Faith in God is based on the premise that there is an absolute; that there are things that are objectively right and objectively wrong. **This causes humanism great distress, since it perceives everything as relative**" (Ekman 71-75).

The Basic goal of Humanism

Enlightening stuff! And it helps to explain the mentality of much of today's society. But in addition to this, if there is no sin, then there is no need for repentance. If there is no need for repentance, then there is no need for salvation and if there is no need for salvation, there is no need for a saviour.

This is the basic goal of humanism, to deny the very need for and existence of our Saviour, the Lord Jesus Christ *(the Son of the living God)*. **In fact, it's the basic centre of** *all-things-anti-Christ.*

In returning to our original point and looking into the balance of everything, as Ulf Ekman said, *"God is objective reality."* He exists and He speaks! Therefore if we want to go about reflecting on what others are saying all the time, that's fine so long as we go beyond what they are saying and hear what God's saying!

We can go to God directly. We are not in the Old Testament, where we need the priest to speak to God or hear Him on our behalf. No! **Each and every one of us can enjoy unbroken fellowship with God.** Yes! He will speak to us through others, and yes we must be teachable to receive revelation that way too. **But this must never replace hearing God for ourselves.**

Yet again God Speaks!

Some believers NEVER hear God for themselves *(which is a major concern to me)*. We must know that our relationship with Him is - *pseudo* - if we never hear Him speak to us except through others. Just as I don't go next door, to hear what my wife wants to say to me, but go directly to my wife and vice-versa. Nor do I go next door and ask them to regurgitate their last meal, so that I can eat it at dinner!

We are not nourished by the exact-same-food that others eat and we must see that our spiritual nutrition must also come to us directly and stop expecting less for our spiritual-well-being, than we do for our physical-well-being!

I would like to conclude this chapter by saying that I have the highest respect for Kenneth E. Hagin, his teaching, which are still widely read today, long after his death, they continue to circle the earth and have left a lasting legacy for Christendom.

Nevertheless, while Hagin preached correctly from Rhema (direct revelation) sadly some of his followers began preaching the logos of his rhema, because they could not hear God for themselves! **They could only rehearse or repeat Hagin's revelation**. It was not direct revelation straight from God, but in-direct revelation. This is not God's best for us. Each of us can enjoy direct revelation.

This is NOT to say that we cannot hear God through others. Otherwise we would not need the five fold ministries that are placed within the Body *"to train and equip the saints for works of service."* **But they only serve the Body - they don't take God's place!**

Instead they teach as God directs and always encourage people to hear God for themselves. If their teaching makes people dependent on their words instead of God's, then something has gone awry!

We must have the courage to hear God and to obey. Bringing to birth what He has said to us individually and corporately. Breakthroughs belong to us through faith in Jesus Christ. Even if the process takes time, like pregnancy, we must have faith in *"...the word of my patience" (Revelation 3:10 KJV).*

❖

CHAPTER 7

Lions of Righteousness!

We must go boldly to the throne of grace, knowing exactly who we are in Christ, confident and knowing what God can do for us. In intercession we approach His throne on behalf of others, so we can't afford to be timid. When we intercede and war against the powers of darkness, it must be done boldly, convinced of the victory that we have in Christ.

> *Let us then approach the throne of grace with <u>confidence</u>, so that we may receive mercy and find grace to help us in our time of need.*
>
> *(Hebrews 4:16)*

> *Let us then **fearlessly and confidently and boldly draw near to the throne of grace** (the throne of God's unmerited favour to us sinners), that we may receive*

71

mercy [for our failures] and find grace to help in good time for every need [appropriate help and well timed help, coming just when we need it].

(AMP)

To defeat the enemy we must be bold and militant. Being militant literally means: having a fighting spirit *(forcefully and uncompromisingly active!)* As believers we have every reason to be bold and militant because we are winners not losers, we are the head and not the tail!

In fact believers need to be more forceful and assertive, because the church is going to have to stand and fight the devil every inch of the way. There seems to be too many laid back Christians. **Laid back Christians don't need armour, just a cushion to lay on!** Believers need to wake up and put on the whole armour of God and take the offensive as good soldiers *(the best defence is always offence!)*

We must NOT be Ignorant

Satan is trying to bring all sorts of corruption into the Church and it is time to fight back. Being led of the Holy Spirit ensures that we are NOT ignorant of Satan's devises. *"To keep Satan from getting the advantage over us; for we are not ignorant of his wiles and intentions"* (2 Corinthians 2:11 AMP).

We do not always have to pray on our knees, we can walk around, run, jump or dance; even wave our arms around if the Spirit leads! But we do need to pray boldly and sometimes loudly, *"the righteous are as bold as a lion"* (Proverbs 28:1b).

Take for instance when a mother feels that her child is in danger, she quite easily *morphs* into a lioness in a split second! She is not concerned at that point with being mild mannered or polite – only with the safety of her offspring! Likewise there is a legitimate reason for our holy fierceness *(righteous indignation)*. We have a job to do. Ministering *(enforcing)* protection to God's people - through prayer.

Besides a lion may not roar all the time, but when he does, it is not softly! It is both loud and *INTIMIDATING!* So let's not be afraid to roar at times, like lions are meant to. We are not timid. In fact it's high time we became intimidating towards our enemy. In all boldness we can raise our voices, with true authority in Christ. *(Nothing however can replace godly character and maturity to increase our boldness, particularly our submission to God's will - see James 4:7).*

We have every right to be bold because we *already* **have the victory in Jesus!** Satan should not be running us around; rather he should be running *from* us, because we are supposed to *already* be more than conquerors!

> *The sting of death is sin, and the power of sin is the law. But thanks be to God!* ***He gives us the victory through our Lord Jesus Christ.***
>
> (1 Corinthians 15:56-57)

> *Now sin is the sting of death, the sin exercises its power [upon the soul] through [the abuse of] the Law. But thanks be to God,* ***who gives us the victory [making us conquerors]*** *through our Lord Jesus Christ.*
>
> (AMP)

Who shall separate us from the love of Christ? Shall trouble or hardship or persecution or famine or nakedness or danger or sword? As it is written: "For your sake we face death all day long; we are considered as sheep to be slaughtered." **No, in all these things we are <u>more than conquerors</u>** *through him who loved us.*

(Romans 8:35-37)

Now, Lord, consider their threats and **enable your servants to speak your word with great boldness.**

(Acts 4:29)

We must operate in Holy Boldness

New Testament Christians were NOT weak and wimpy but strong and enduring. Persecution did not hinder their vision in any way. John the Baptist came boldly proclaiming to King Herod and the Chief Priests *"Repent! for the Kingdom of God is at hand."* His words were not filled with weak religious phrases, his message was clear, bold, blasting and to the point. He gave the Word of God boldly!

The New Testament message is the same for everyone, for the powerful, the weak, the rich, the poor, the famous and the unknown. It is the same for everyone. It should not matter what town or church we are from, the message is the same.

Boldness needs to come back into the Church and the fear of retaliation must leave. We must be God pleasers and not men pleasers! Boldly preaching God's Word without any compromise. **We need boldness to proclaim that our faith in God works.**

Confess to one another therefore your faults (your slips, your false steps, your offenses, your sins) and pray [also] for one another, that you may be healed and restored [to a spiritual tone of mind and heart]. **The earnest (heartfelt, continued) prayer of a righteous man makes tremendous power available [dynamic in its working].**

(James 5:16 AMP)

We must have fervency to push-through and a desire to see results. We must also labour for people to come through to maturity, standing in the gap for them.

Epaphras, who is one of yourselves, a servant of Christ Jesus, sends you greetings. [He is] **always striving for you earnestly in his prayers,** *[pleading] that you may [as* **persons of ripe character and clear conviction]** **stand firm and mature** *[in spiritual growth], convinced and fully assured in everything willed by God.*

(Colossians 4:12 AMP)

❖

CHAPTER 8

Warring in Prophecy

W

e aught to have a strong desire to prophesy over our own lives, the lives of others, including the atmosphere. **When we prophesy, we are speaking forth the very will of God,** into a situation and literally speaking strength and encouragement into people's lives. *"Everyone who prophesies speaks to men for their **strengthening, encouragement and comfort"** (1 Corinthians 14:3).*

> *This charge I commit unto thee, son Timothy, **according to the prophecies which went before on thee, that thou by them mightest war a good warfare;** Holding faith, and a good conscience; which some having put away concerning faith have made shipwreck.*
>
> *(1 Timothy 1:18-19 KJV)*

When we receive prophecies we must take hold of them by the Spirit and speak them out. Travailing with groanings, praying over them in tongues, keeping them alive in our spirits. **We must continue to do this until the prophecy** *(revealed will of God for our lives)* **comes into manifestation.**

Prophecy always involves NOW-FAITH

We have to accept that there is a definite time-scale and season for the maturity and manifestation of any prophecy. Although God may have said it to us *now (and has our faith filled cooperation now)*, still we must persevere in the foreseeable-now! Meaning that the day we receive a prophecy, is not necessarily the *same* day it's going to be fulfilled!

In fact walking-and-living-out prophecy can take considerable time. Some prophecies will even out-live us entirely by seeing their fulfilment in the next generation!

Nevertheless each step - of any vision or plan - must be taken by faith. Sadly many prophecies/visions are abandoned. Not because people have not believed in them, rather because they have failed to persevere during the outworking of such prophesies.

The fact is this, very often when God *speaks* - the exact opposite seems to happen! Take David for instance, from the Old Testament, who was anointed King yet still spent a number of years living in a cave with a bunch of disgruntled outcasts and misfits!

Modern day Example

A more modern day example could be Nelson Mandela; who politically had a vision yet in order to stand-up for his ideals, he became a political prisoner for 27 long years. Almost three decades behind bars, most of which was spent on Robben Island (South Africa) - in the same cell!

New Testament Example

Paul our New Testament example – on his way to Rome was beaten and imprisoned, shipwrecked and bitten by a snake! Yet *still* he acted in accordance with his goal, including issuing words of knowledge to his captors - warning them so everyone could escape shipwreck!

> **NOW _faith_** - *is the substance of things hoped for, the evidence of things not seen.*
>
> *(Hebrews 11:1 KJV)*

With this level of perseverance in mind we must *take-hold* of prophecy by faith in the **continuous-now** *"...calling those things which be not as though they were"* *(Romans 4:17 KJV)*. **As we do this, we actively agree with and boldly declare our faith in God's revealed will for our lives - regardless of time**.

The God kind of faith is always **"now-faith"** – so whether it takes decades or not - our faith in God's prophetic Word must always be activated - right NOW!

The Authorised says it like this; and please note that the emphasis and implication is in *"...WHAT **WE** SAY,"* simply because once God has spoken, the rest is down to us!

*Have faith in God. For verily I __say__ unto you, That whosoever shall __say__ unto this mountain, Be thou removed, and be thou cast into the sea; and shall not doubt in his heart, but shall **believe that those things which he __saith__ shall come to pass: he shall have whatsoever he __saith__.***

(Mark 11:22-24 KJV)

It's obvious then, that there is power in what __we speak__ into the atmosphere. Therefore we must equally remember that, *"Death and life are in the power of the tongue" (Proverbs 18:21)*. King David also said, *"I have believed therefore I have spoken..." (Psalm 116:10a KJV)* **Just like David, we too must give *voice* to our faith and not unbelief!**

Salvation involves *believing with our __hearts__* and *confessing with our __mouths__* that Jesus Christ is Lord. Our words and our thoughts must measure up. Faith in Christ does not just consist of hollow words, but the thoughts and the intents of our hearts are also very influential, *" ...as a man **thinks** in his heart, so is he..." (Proverbs 23:7a NKJV)*

The exciting part is this; that when our mouths and hearts reach agreement – there is power – that's when we see results, *(too many people are in division with themselves!)* Our whole beings must be caught up with Christ. Our whole lives *(spirit, soul and body)*. This is true salvation.

His Words are Spirit and Life

It is crucial that we *continue* speaking the Word of God *(rhema AND logos)* over our lives - **for the *rest* of our lives!** Jesus said in John 6:63, *"the words that I speak unto you, they* *are spirit, and they are life" (KJV)*. **Prophecy isn't just to be spoken out once, but over and over until it manifests.**

We are to labour with prophecy in the spirit, so that God's *revealed-will* can be *"...done on earth as it is in Heaven."* His will *must* come to pass. His Word does NOT return to Him void *(Isaiah 55:11)*.

Esther was called to the Kingdom *"...for such a time as this."* In other words, it was no mistake that she was *positioned* perfectly to help her own people. She was not there to enjoy the palace opulence, spending her days in luxury and ease! It was a crisis that she had been equipped for and could not rescue herself from. Instead it was through her uncle Mordecai, that the Spirit of God warned Esther by saying:

> **Think not with thyself that thou shalt escape** *in the king's house, more than all the Jews. For if thou altogether holdest thy peace at this time, then shall there enlargement and* **deliverance arise to the Jews from another place**... *but thou and thy father's house shall be destroyed: and who knoweth whether* **thou art come to the kingdom for such a time as this?**
>
> *(Esther 4:13b-14 KJV)*

Mordecai prophesied that God would raise up another to stand in the gap for the Jews if she didn't. **Esther recognised that her uncle Mordecai was speaking by the Spirit and authority of God** *"...thus saith the Lord!"* Resulting in her *volition* to put her own life on the line - for her people - in accordance with God's Word. She trusted and obeyed and came-out-on-top!

Called to Meditate

Now let's go to Joshua chapter 1 verse 8. In most translations of the bible, such as: The Authorised *(KJV)*, New Jerusalem *(NJB)*, Amplified *(AMP)*, and the New International Version *(NIV)* - just to name a few - the word **MEDITATE** is used.

> *This book of the law shall not depart out of thy mouth; but thou shalt* **"*meditate*"** *therein day and night, that thou mayest observe to do according to all that is written therein: for* **then thou shalt make thy way prosperous, and then thou shalt have good success.**
>
> *(Joshua 1:8 KJV)*

To make a brief word study here, let's take a closer look at this word to **"*meditate*"** - using the Vine's Expository Dictionary and the Strong's Exhaustive Concordance. We will discover its original Hebrew meaning, at the time it was first written. It certainly had some very interesting meanings!

The Hebrew word for **"*meditate*"** used here in verse 8 of Joshua chapter 1 is: *Hagah* daw-gaw' 1897 hagah a primitive root *(compare 1901)*; **to murmur** *(in pleasure or anger)*; by implication, **to ponder:--imagine, meditate, mourn, mutter, roar**, X sore, **speak, study, talk, utter**.

This puts a new light on things! For example in the English language *"to meditate"* is commonly understood as simply: *thinking hard about something, reflection or deep concentration.* To be exact, the Concise Oxford Dictionary simply says that to meditate is: *"to plan mentally, design, exercise the mind and contemplation."* This gives no sense of *noise* at all, more of tranquillity and passivity - but certainly not *"roaring!"*

The Oxford Guide to the English language adds that to meditate means: *"to think deeply and to quietly plan."* However these short definitions seem only to involve the *mind* – whereas meditation from a biblical point of view has much more activity! In fact it involves the entire person – spirit, soul and body.

To be clear, the biblical purpose for meditation is not akin with new age techniques such as *positive-thinking or mind-over-matter exercises!* True biblical meditation is never humanistic or carnal in any way but is a life style that is *regularly* encouraged or inspired by the Holy Spirit.

Now to quote the Vine's Expository Dictionary: *"Hagah (1897), 'to meditate, moan, growl, utter, speak.' This word is common to both ancient and modern Hebrew... Hagah also expresses the 'growl' of lions (Isaiah 32:4) and the 'mourning' of doves (Isaiah 38:14)."*

> *Therefore will I **howl** for Moab, and I will **cry out** for all Moab; mine heart shall **mourn** for the men of Kir-heres.*
> *(Jeremiah 48:31 KJV)*

Growl, Roar, Moan and Speak

We have to ask ourselves concerning meditation, when the Holy Spirit inspired the writing of the scripture, was He solely instructing us to project some form of *"human-mental-assent"* towards His Word or were we to get much more involved? If so, does He actually expect us to *growl, roar, moan and speak* over the scriptures, even day and night – just like He instructed Joshua?

The answer to this must be a clear and bold, "Yes!" Because scripture has not morphed into something more politically correct since it was written! Actually boldness is our biblical right. Proverbs 28:1 says, *"The Righteous are as Bold as a Lion" (Jesus is the Lion of Judah!)*

Our growl has authority and as we travail over the scriptures and the prophecies that God has given to us personally and corporately, they *will* come to pass. And before this causes any of us to go tilt – all we are talking about here - is bringing the will of God to birth in our lives. Activating our faith by speaking out God's Word boldly and authoritatively. I am not suggesting for a moment that just because we roar God's Word back to Him, it will come to pass!

No! But we *are* talking about speaking God's Word with authority over our own lives. This is a form of meditation. Meditation as seen in the original Hebrew language then is not just mental ponderings *(as our English language restricts it)* – but involves projecting our faith, in ways that are audible, fervent and verbal. *(Includes various expressions of the Spirit as mentioned in previous chapters).*

It all Sounds the Same to Me!

Without vision we perish. We must see Jesus as our faithful High Priest, who takes our confessions *(meditations)* in agreement with His Word and brings them to pass. He *performs* His Word *(2 Chronicles 10:15 KJV).*

In terms of *righteous indignation* let's go back to the Strong's definition for *"**meditate**"* – where we also saw the word *ANGER* in there: *"(1897), hagah, (Hebrew)* **to murmur** *(***in pleasure *or anger**); …to ponder:- imagine, meditate, mourn, mutter, **roar**, sore, **speak**, study, talk, utter."* We saw Jesus sighing with *righteous indignation (anger)* at the tomb of Lazarus, due to the unbelief of the crowd.

We must desire to know the heart of God, such as Jehoshaphat who was a man of great wealth and honour. King Ahab wanted Jehoshaphat to join forces with him against Ramoth Gilead. Jehoshaphat wanted to help Ahab, but **he first desired to seek counsel from the Lord**. Even though he made a mistake, God knew his heart.

In the war against Moab and Ammon and their vast armies, **Jehoshaphat wanted to hear from God, to be obedient to His *voice*,** so when Jahaziel prophesied, Jehoshaphat was careful to listen.

> *Do not be afraid or discouraged because of this vast army for the battle is not yours, but God's.* Tomorrow *march down against them. They will be climbing up by the Pass of Ziz, and you will find them at the end of the gorge in the Desert of Jeruel.*
>
> *You will not have to fight this battle. Take up your positions; stand firm and see the deliverance the Lord will give you, O Judah and Jerusalem. Do not be afraid, do not be discouraged. Go out to face them tomorrow, and the Lord will be with you.*
>
> (2 Chronicles 20:15b-17)

Jehoshaphat recognised God's voice; he *recognised* that the words coming from Jahaziel were from God, and he knew that no matter how foolish, in the natural these words sounded, he *had* to obey them. Jehoshaphat and his people fell down in *worship* before the Lord.

Jehoshaphat took hold of the Spoken Words. He did not just sit on them, thinking about them. He got his people together, told them to have faith in the words of the prophet. Jehoshaphat sent men ahead of his army singing and worshipping God. As God had promised not one of his men had to fight, because when they approached the enemy, they were all dead.

We must do likewise. When we receive a prophecy from God we should get hold of it by faith, continually speaking out those words by faith. Only then will we see the prophecy come to pass.

Just as Jehoshaphat put actions to the prophecy by being obedient and trusting God, we too must take hold of prophecies. **We must put our faith into ACTION.** Our battle is a spiritual one. Spiritual warfare we cannot avoid! Much will be brought to birth in the spirit realm, when we completely trust God that His promises will come to pass.

Strong and Courageous

Jahaziel told them not to be afraid or discouraged:

Be strong and courageous. **Do not be afraid or discouraged** *because of the king of Assyria and the vast army with him,* **for there is a greater power with us** *than with him. With him is only the arm of flesh but with us is the Lord our God to help us and to fight our battles.*

(2 Chronicles 32:7-8a)

Prophecies are for strength and encouragement. When we pray and engage in spiritual warfare, travailing over them *(prophecy)*, angels are sent out on our behalf, to destroy the activity of the enemy.

*King Hezekiah and the prophet Isaiah son of Amoz cried out in prayer to heaven about this. **And the Lord sent an angel, who annihilated all the fighting men** and the leaders and officers in the camp of the Assyrian king.*

(2 Chronicles 32:20-21a)

The victory is ours, the battle is the Lord's.

❖

CHAPTER 9

Binding and Loosing

The bible tells us to "pray always with all prayer and supplication in the Spirit, being watchful to this end with all perseverance and supplication for all the saints." The Amplified Bible takes this a step further:

Pray at all times - on every occasion in every season - in the Spirit, with all manner of prayers and entreaty. To that end keep alert and watch with strong purpose and perseverance, interceding on behalf of all the saints - God's consecrated people.

(Ephesians 6:18 AMP)

Prayer is part of our armour. We need to know how to pray with all different types of prayer and in different situations, because different prayers have different rules.

There is divine order in prayer; we must ask the Holy Spirit how to tackle each situation.

The bible makes it quite clear that Jesus has given us the power to bind and loose in reference to Satan and his cohorts. When we were given the *"keys"* of the Kingdom, God was giving us back the authority that was lost at the time of Adam.

We have the authority to bind and to loose; we have that right, and what we bind on earth shall be bound in heaven. *"I tell you the truth, whatever you bind on earth will be bound in heaven, and whatever you loose on earth will be loosed in heaven" (Matthew 18:18).*

Rise up in Power

As Christians, we need to wake up and realise that we have the **power and the authority** in the Name of the Lord Jesus Christ to bind the powers of the devil and to loose |those afflicted, which Satan put into captivity. It is not a matter of us crying, *"Oh God do something; the devil is giving me such a hard time."* We need to rise up in the power and authority given us and tell the devil where to go!

> *Let the saints rejoice in this honour and sing for joy on their beds. May the praise of God be in their mouths and **a double-edged sword in their hands,** to inflict vengeance on the nations and punishment on the peoples, **to bind** their kings with fetters, their nobles with shackles of iron, **to carry out the sentence written against them**. This is the glory of all his saints.*
>
> *(Psalm 149:5-9)*

BIND [deo] means: Tie, seal, constrain, confine, detain, restrict, forbid or prohibit, improper and unlawful.

LOOSE [luo] means: Unfasten, detach, disconnect, to free, to liberate, to release, to unbind, to undo, to dissolve.

For us to be effective we must understand what is going on in the spirit realm. The spirit-realm is the origin of ALL things: victory, healing, deliverance, peace, wisdom, joy, every need originates from here. **When we pray, God's power is at work backing our prayers. It is God's power that does the work through prayer.**

Disarm the Strongman

Jesus told us that whatever is bound or loosed by the believer is done on the basis that it has already been done in heaven, by the Lord Himself. Jesus disarmed powers and authorities, making a public spectacle of them; He triumphed over them on the Cross *(Colossians 2:15)*. Jesus came to destroy the works of the devil *(1 John 3:8)*. Satan is the strong man of the house and he needs to be bound and disarmed.

*But when the Pharisees heard this, they said, "It is only by Beelzebub, the prince of demons, that this fellow drives out demons." Jesus knew their thoughts and said to them, "**Every kingdom divided against itself will be ruined, and every city or household divided against itself will not stand.***

91

If Satan drives out Satan, he is divided against himself. How then can his kingdom stand? And if I drive out demons by Beelzebub, by whom do your people drive them out? So then, they will be your judges.

*But if I **drive out demons by the Spirit of God**, then the kingdom of God has come upon you. Or again, **how can anyone enter a strong man's house and carry off his possessions unless he first ties up the strong man?** Then he can rob his house. He who is not with me is against me, and he who does not gather with me scatters."*
(Matthew 12:24-30)

Taking back the Stolen Goods

We must bind the strongman, enter his territory and take back the things he has stolen. As believers in Christ Jesus, God provides all that we need. The enemy tries to keep our blessings bound *(Daniel 10:13)* but it is our duty to loose those things in the authority we have in Christ. The enemy has loosed death, destruction, sickness and poverty including much more.

We must take our place and bind what needs to be bound and loose what needs to be loosed, by speaking out God's Word and His promises. Note: When "binding" also make sure to "loose" the blessings of God! We must be led of the Spirit because He knows what is going on and will give us His wisdom and direction.

Authority is the key representing ownership. Jesus gave us the keys of heaven and we have rightful ownership! In Matthew 12:22-37, Jesus cast evil spirits out but afterwards the religious authorities challenged His authority. They accused Him of doing it by the power of Beelzebub *(verse 24)* but Jesus was the key, who held the keys of the Kingdom. Those keys have been given to us.

Angels ready to Work

We must realise our power of command, and command things in the spirit realm to be loosed or bound. We have this authority in the Name of Jesus. Angels have their role to play. They are put at our disposal, and we need to acknowledge the fact that we have hundreds of angels waiting for us to put them to work!

> Bless *(affectionately, gratefully praise)* the Lord, you His angels, you mighty ones who do His commandments, **hearkening to the _voice_ of His word**. Bless *(affectionately, gratefully praise)* the Lord, all you His hosts, you His ministers who do His pleasure.
>
> *(Psalm 103:20-21 AMP)*

However our attitude towards the ministry of angels must not be flippant. As the scripture above reveals, angels harken *(listen)* to the voice of God's Word (even when His saints speak it) and **cannot be put to work on the basis of anything else, other than God's Word.** However saints all over the world are speaking His Word today. WE ARE THE VOICE OF HIS WORD. As we release it into the atmosphere by faith - angels can then respond. *(They "...obey His Word" NIV) "...to do HIS bidding and HIS pleasure" (verse 21 NIV + KJV).*

Angels are servants, who can only pay attention to us when we speak God's Word! They can't act according to anything else. Likewise when we fail to speak God's Word, we hinder their activity. Speaking the Word releases them to do what they were originally commissioned to do. *"Are not the angels all ministering spirits (servants) sent out in the service [of God for the assistance] of those who are to inherit salvation?"* (Hebrews 1:14 AMP)

Satan assigns Demons

Let's be clear about this, Satan assigns demons; it is they whom we bind - NOT Satan himself. Jesus will eventually bind the devil when He returns. But we can put constant pressure on the enemy by ENFORCING the victory that Christ already won for us!

It's essential though that we understand that we are NOT binding *people (only the spirits influencing them or within them!)* Prayer is NOT voodoo, where we manipulate other people's lives. We cannot operate like that. We can't even "bind" their sin; only their own repentance can deal with that! We must never try and play God.

Another point: We do *not* loose spirits either! We can't loose them from their assignments simply because we never commissioned their assignments! We are not here to loose demons, only to bind them. It says in Psalm 105:21-22, *"He made Joseph lord of his house and ruler of all his substance, **to bind his princes** at his pleasure and teach his elders wisdom."*

Let me emphasise this point so that extremes can be avoided. The Old Testament was a type and a shadow. IN

THE NEW TESTAMENT WE LOOSE PEOPLE AND BIND ONLY DEMONS! If we ever begin thinking that our job is to loose demons *(in any context)*, this would be synonymous with witchcraft!

At the tomb of Lazarus Jesus said, *"<u>Loose</u> him and let him go" (John 11:44).* **Jesus demonstrated to us through this event, that our ministry is to people *(not to demons)* and to help the captives go free!** In fact the same spirit and anointing that rested upon Jesus rests upon us. Isaiah said of Jesus, *"The Spirit of the Lord GOD is upon me; because the LORD hath anointed me... **to proclaim liberty to the captives, and the opening of the prison to them that are bound..."*** *(Isaiah 61:1 KJV)*

So what does *"loosing"* refer to in Matthew 18:18? Loosing refers to: SETTING THE CAPTIVE FREE and RELEASING THE WILL OF GOD *("...on earth as it is in heaven" Matthew 6:10).* It is the year of the Lord's favour! God wants to lavish His "favour" through us. His extravagant love. Isaiah continued in verse 2,

> ***To proclaim the year of the Lord's favour...*** *to comfort all who mourn, and provide for those who grieve in Zion - to bestow on them a crown of beauty instead of ashes, the oil of gladness instead of mourning and **a garment of praise instead of a spirit of despair...***
>
> *(Isaiah 61:1-3)*

Or as the KJV puts it, *"the garment of praise for the spirit of heaviness."*

Many captives will go free! Through this ministry that the Lord has bestowed upon us *(of setting the captives free)* we will see many released from the yolk of enslavement, which Satan has put around them. Isaiah 10:27 says, *"…it shall come to pass in that day, that his burden shall be taken away from off thy shoulder, and his yoke from off thy neck, and* **the yoke shall be destroyed because of the anointing."**

Loosed from Infirmity

Now Jesus was teaching in one of the synagogues on the Sabbath. And there was a woman there who **for eighteen years had had an infirmity caused by a spirit (a demon of sickness).** *She was bent completely forward and utterly unable to straighten herself up or to look upward.*

And when Jesus saw her, He called [her to Him] and said to her, **Woman, you are <u>released</u> from your infirmity!** *Then He laid [His] hands on her, and instantly she was made straight, and she recognized and thanked and praised God.*

(Luke 13:10-13 AMP)

The NIV says, *"… **set free** from your infirmity."*

The ruler of the synagogue became angry over this deliverance because it was done on the Sabbath *(note: legalism will always challenge our right to freedom!)*

Jesus answered,

You hypocrites! Doesn't each of you on the Sabbath untie his ox or donkey from the stall and lead it out to give it water? Then should not this woman, a daughter of Abraham, whom **Satan has kept bound** *for eighteen years,* **be set free** *on the Sabbath day* **from what bound her?***

(Luke 13:15-16)

Freed from Death

Lazarus was loosed. God has given us this same authority to loose people from death, spiritually and physically.

Then they took away the stone from the place where the dead was laid. And Jesus lifted up his eyes, and said, Father, I thank thee that thou hast heard me. And I knew that thou hearest me always: but because of the people which stand by I said it, that they may believe that thou hast sent me.

And when he thus had spoken, **he cried with a loud voice, Lazarus, come forth.** *And he that was dead came forth, bound hand and foot with grave clothes: and his face was bound about with a napkin.* **Jesus saith unto them, Loose him, and let him go.**

(John 11:41-44 KJV)

The exact same Greek word is used for "loose" in both cases. "**Loose** him and let him go" *(John 11:44 KJV)* and "...whatever you **loose** on earth" *(Matthew 18:18 KJV).*

Strong's #3089 luo loo'-o a primary verb; to **"loosen"** *(literally or figuratively)*:--**break *(up)*, destroy, dissolve, *(un-)*loose, melt, put off.**

The Greek word for "loose" in the text is [luo] *(W.E. Vine)*. Denotes:

- To loose anything bound or fastened
- To loose one bound
- To release
- To put off
- To free from bondage or disease, one held by Satan, by restoration to health. *(Luke 13:16)*

Bind the Strongman

It is important to remember, that in situations where Satan's *"strongman"* has been appointed over individuals, homes, churches, cites, or nations, we as the Church of Jesus Christ have the authority to bind the strongman and to liberate the people involved.

Again it is important always to remember that "binding" refers to Satan's powers and demons, whereas "loosing" applies only to people who have been bound by the forces of darkness. SATAN'S POWERS ARE BOUND BUT THE VICTIMS ARE LOOSED! This is what happens in spiritual warfare as the result of effective prayer *(see James 5:16 AMP)*.

Paul E. Billheimer wrote: "The most important activity is *'Pray without ceasing' (1 Thessalonians 5:17)*. A suggested paraphrase of this passage is: *'Make prayer the main business of your life.'* With exceptions, through the centuries, the church has never taken prayer seriously. Few of us take it seriously today.

For the most part, prayer has been and still is window dressing, a sort of ritualistic or cosmetic exercise. The church at large, and most of us individually use prayer as a slave to our conscience – that is, we pray enough to keep our conscience from barking too loudly!"

He went on to say,

"If the church will not pray - God will not act. God never goes over the head of His church to enforce His decision. He will not take things out of her hands. To do so would sabotage His training program.

Another way of putting it could be that ...*God will not be accused of usurping the Authority that He has bestowed upon his own Body!* Therefore it is detrimental that we co-operate *(with the Spirit of God)* then, so that the will of God comes to pass in the earth. Matthew 6:10 says, *'Thy will be done on earth as it is in heaven.'*

Only by bearing this overwhelming weight of responsibility can the bride be brought to her full stature as co-sovereign of the universe. This is the reason that when she fails God will wait. This is why He will do nothing in the realm of human redemption until she accepts her responsibility and uses her privilege and prerogative of intercession" (Billheimer 52).

God does not move without Prayer

John Wesley said, "God will do nothing but in answer to prayer." **S. D. Gordon** said, "The greatest thing anyone can do for God and for man is to pray. Prayer is striking the winning blow, service is gathering up the result." **E.M. Bounds** said: "God shapes the world by prayer. The more praying there is in the world, the better the world will be, the mightier the forces against evil."

If these things are true, then surely prayer should be the main business of the day.

❖

CHAPTER 10

Prayer of Agreement

When praying the prayer of agreement there has to be a similar or equal level of faith involved; this means the fewer the people involved the better! This type of prayer is easier when just two or three join their faith together to approach the throne of grace; simply because there is more chance of praying in total agreement.

- **Agree** - to harmonise, same opinion, approve, conform, match

- **Agreement** - accordance, compliance, concord

It suffices to say that the prayer-of-agreement needs "agreement" for it to work! *(See Amos 3:3 "Can two walk together, except they be agreed?")*

Again, I tell you that if two of you on earth agree about anything you ask for, it shall be done for you by my Father in heaven. For where two or three come together in my name, there am I with them.

(Matthew 18:19-20)

Having prayed together we must remain in faith and one accord, until the answer comes. It helps having someone join their faith with ours, as this provides a joint force, to push back powers of darkness and for taking hold of the victory.

You will pursue your enemies, and they will fall by the sword before you. Five of you will chase a hundred, and a hundred of you will chase ten thousand, and your enemies will fall by the sword before you.

(Leviticus 26:7-8)

One person can only do so much, but if we join forces with the Holy Spirit and take authority, the enemy is put to flight.

How could one man chase a thousand or two put ten thousand to flight, unless their Rock had sold them, unless the Lord had given them up?

(Deuteronomy 32:30)

How could one single enemy chase a thousand of them, and two put ten thousand to flight, unless the Lord had destroyed them?

(Deuteronomy 32:30 TLB)

Love is a Powerful Force

The more people there are, the more work will be done. When we join forces together, we deal with the enemy more swiftly than if there is just one person. *"Love"* is a strong element in the Prayer of Agreement and is a mighty weapon when we stand in faith against Satan, in love for our brothers and sisters.

The Blood of Jesus binds us together in love. It is a mighty weapon and a powerful force, especially when husbands and wives come together in agreement. This is really powerful in the spirit realm, *(because of their joint covenant).*

Jesus is with us in the midst of our "agreement" to sanctify it and put His seal of approval on it. He is also our mediator, our High Priest and presents our requests to the Father.

- Covenant: - to agree, make pact, bond and treaty

Take this most seriously: A yes on earth is yes in heaven; a no on earth is no in heaven. **What you say to one another is eternal.** *I mean this. When two of you get together on anything at all on earth and make a prayer of it, my Father in heaven goes into action. And when two or three of you are together because of me, you can be sure that I'll be there.*

(Matthew 18:19-20 MSG)

Jesus will sanction our agreement and add His agreement to ours. Then as our High Priest He will "mediate" on our behalf - to present our requests to the Father. We are not gathered together in our own name, but in the Name of Jesus Christ, to glorify Him. Jesus Christ is the High Priest; He mediates on our behalf.

United we Stand, Divided we Fall

The Prayer of Agreement unites us in the Spirit. We become one voice in the spirit, not a whisper but a mighty roar. *"They all joined together constantly in prayer..." (Acts 1:14a)*

The disciples were constantly united when they prayed and joined forces in the Spirit. *"Now when the Day of Pentecost had fully come, they were all with **one accord** in once place" (Acts 2:1 NKJV).*

For people to be in ONE place and of ONE mind is a miracle in itself! *"If ye have bitter envying and strife in your hearts, glory not, and lie not against the truth... For **where envying and strife is, there is confusion and every evil work"** (James 3:14,16).* Note: strife is angry bitter disagreement, contention, factions and division.

Discord does not bring Blessings

Their faith was joined together and they stayed in one accord until the answer came.

> *And they, when they heard it, **lifted their voices together with one united mind** to God and said, O Sovereign Lord, You are he who made the heaven and the earth and the sea and everything that is in them.*
> *(Acts 4:24 AMP)*

The fullness of God will not come until we are in *"one accord."* It is not easy to be in agreement, the devil will attack with division and doubt, but we must fight the enemy and be in one accord.

*So the soldiers, carrying out their orders, took Paul
with them during the night and brought him as far as
Antipatris. The next day they let the cavalry go on with
him, while they returned to the barracks.*

(Acts 23:31-32)

They were bold and the place was filled with the power
of the Holy Spirit. *"So Peter was kept in prison, but the church
was earnestly praying to God for him" (Acts 12:5).*

Constant Prayer

The church was in constant prayer for Peter, they were
determined and never doubted that he would be released
and not killed.

*The night before Herod was to bring him to trail, Peter
was sleeping between two soldiers, bound with two chains,
and sentries stood guard at the entrance. Suddenly an
angel of the Lord appeared and a light shone in the cell.
He struck Peter on the side and woke him up "Quick get
up!" he said, and the chains fell off Peter's wrists. Then
the angel said to him, "Put on your clothes and sandals."
And Peter did so.*

(Acts 12:6-8a)

Even though Peter was bound and surrounded by
soldiers, the angel released him.

*When this had dawned on him, he went to the house of
Mary the mother of John, also called Mark, where many
people had gathered and were praying. Peter knocked at*

*the outer entrance, and a servant girl name Rhoda came
to answer the door.*

(Acts 12:12-13)

**The people continued praying until their prayers
were answered and Peter was released.** When we pray in
agreement and unity – ONLY then we will see many mighty
things happen. We must not allow doubt to come in, because
doubt hinders what we are standing in faith for. *In fact if
we are in doubt at all, then we are not in faith!* We must
not become doubtful about what we are praying for.

**If we stand in faith, and believe, our prayers WILL
come to pass.**

❖

CHAPTER 11

Prayer of Commitment

One of the prayers mentioned in the bible is *"the prayer of commitment,"* or *"casting your cares upon the Lord"* (*in other words turning cares into prayers!*)

Casting the whole of your care, [all you anxieties, all your worries, all your concerns, once and for all] on Him, for He cares for you affectionately, and cares about you watchfully.

(1 Peter 5:7 AMP)

Do not be anxious about anything, but in everything, but prayer and petition, with thanksgiving, present your requests to God.

(Philippians 4:6)

Worry cannot trust God

Worrying about things does not change the circumstances, but it can make us ill. It is a fact today, that there are many people physically sick and in hospitals all over the world, because of worry! Graveyards are full of people who died prematurely because of worry. It did not help them in their situations; in fact worry and concern killed them before their time.

So refuse to worry, get into that place of faith, knowing that the **Lord Jesus is in control**. Only faith in Christ can dispel the worries and concerns that we carry around.

Greater is He that is in you than he that is in the world.
(1 John 4:4 KJV)

Worry is a Needless Burden

When we worry it is like carrying a heavy sack and no matter where we go we carry it with us. Many people get down on their knees and pray for the burden to be lifted, but as soon as they have finished their prayer, they pick up the sack again.

No! Leave it there. *"Cast the whole of your care... once and for all on Him" (1 Peter 5:7; Philippians 4:6).* This is what the bible says, so we must *refuse* to worry.

It is easy enough to practise the second part of the verse *"in everything by prayer and petition with thanksgiving present your requests unto God,"* but this part is not going to work without taking the first step, *"do not be anxious about* ***anything!"***

In order to stop holding onto cares and anxieties we must ask ourselves the following questions: *Am I fretting? Am I suffering with anxiety, cares or concern?*

If the answer is, "Yes, all the time," then the next step must be, "Lord I am putting this (name it) into your hands. I REFUSE to fret or worry anymore. I REFUSE to be unduly concerned. You care for me affectionately and watchfully. Help me to renew my mind concerning this, in Jesus name amen." This actively turns all of our cares into prayers!

Jesus tells us in Matthew 6:25-34, that we are not to worry about our lives, what to eat, drink, or put on. Jesus goes on to say,

> *Therefore I tell you, do not worry about your life, what you will eat or drink; or about your body, what you will wear. Is not life more important than food, and the body more important than clothes? Look at the birds of the air; they do not sow or reap or store away in barns, and yet your heavenly Father feeds them. Are you not much more valuable than they?* **Who of you by worrying can add a single hour to his life?**
>
> (Matthew 6:25-27)

Worry opens the door to Torment

This prayer of commitment is important for our physical and spiritual lives. By using this prayer we can stay free from worry, concerns and the bondages of fear. **Allowing ourselves to worry opens the door for Satan to attack and torment us.** We must pray for the fruits of the Spirit to manifest in our lives (*Galatians 5:22-23*).

God does not want us to live in worry or fear:

*Cast **all** your anxiety on him because he cares for you. Be self-controlled and alert. Your enemy the devil prowls around like a roaring lion looking for someone to devour. Resist him, standing firm in the faith...*
                                            (1 Peter 5:7-9)

For this reason I remind you to fan into flame the gift of God, which is in you through the laying on of my hands. For God did not give us a spirit of timidity, but a spirit of power, of love and of self-discipline.
                                            (2 Timothy 1:6-7)

Renewing our thought Lives

God's love has equipped us with the gifts of the Holy Spirit. We must constantly renew our minds, fanning them up and using the gifts that are within us.

*Do not be conformed to this world (this age), [fashioned after and adapted to its external, superficial customs], but **be transformed (changed) by the [entire] renewal of your mind [by its new ideals and its new attitude]**, so that you may prove [for yourselves] what is the good and acceptable and perfect will of God, even the thing which is good and acceptable and perfect [in His sight for you].*
                                            (Romans 12:2 AMP)

If we want to see God's good and perfect will out worked in our lives, first we must discipline and renew our minds. How? By adapting our minds to the Word of God. We must put on the *"helmet of salvation"* to guard our minds and no longer think like the world thinks.

The world's ways are dis-interesting to those who have their helmets fully fitted! It's those who constantly take it off and put it back on again who are having problems. James 1:8 says that a "...*double minded* man is unstable in **all** his ways." *(Greek for "double-minded" – Strong's #1374 dipsuchos dip'-soo-khos from 1364 and 5590; __two-spirited__, i.e. vacillating [in opinion or purpose]:--double minded.)*

Anything can be *mechanical* at first but a disciplined mind eventually sees change. We are naturally and carnally speaking, creatures of habit! We must make the Word of God our habit, just as Smith Wigglesworth was remembered for – every 15 minutes he would get his bible out no matter where he was or who he was with, and begin to read it out loud!

That might seem extreme to some, but the bible says that we know them by their fruits and this man certainly left a legacy of fruit and rich inspiring testimonies that are still helping others overcome today! *(Revelation 12:11)*

Exchange your Thinking

We literally MUST exchange our way of thinking – for His *(Isaiah 55:8-9)*. The bible declares that we have the Mind of Christ. Not *"will have"* but *"have"* the mind of Christ. The same way that we *"are"* healed by His stripes, and not *"going-to-be"* healed by His stripes. We *"are"* the righteousness of God in Christ Jesus; right now - not *"one-day-in-the-future!"* It all applies right now – by faith.

As we change our thinking, a process takes place – a transforming process, where the Holy Spirit expresses the divine nature through us. *"For as he thinketh in his heart, so is* he…" *(Proverbs 23:7a KJV)* So instead of saying, *"We are what we eat"* we need so say, *"We are what we think!"* Because when our *minds* change, WE change!

God Himself cannot be accused of *usurping* our free will. A man can *decide* to think as he pleases, but not all forms of thinking will do us any good or bring us harmony. Only Christ has the peace that passes understanding. Change takes place – according to the Word of God. We are transformed into what God intends for our lives. Jesus made this transformation possible by the cross. Today we must allow the Holy Spirit to process our minds according to the mind of Christ – the WORD!

Our minds can be our worst enemy at times, even for years! However right-thinking *alone* does not bring salvation, *(by grace through faith).* For example there will be people in heaven who accepted Christ as their Lord and Saviour during old age – who never got the chance to really walk in victory during their lifetime or even experience God's will for their lives.

Yet this did not stop them receiving God's saving grace. Their minds may not have been perfectly renewed by His Word *(through the process of sanctification)* but perfection was never a requirement for salvation. It is free! Yet to *walk* with Christ there is much that is required and involves renewing our minds daily.

So yes we are saved by grace, regardless of an undisciplined mind, but I dare say that *most* Christians are still focussed on negatives, just as much as they ever were!

As a result many believers are still living defeated lives simply because of *stinking-thinking* and a refusal to discipline their minds.

The Triumphant Church

Kenneth E. Hagin wrote in his book, "The Triumphant Church - *Dominion Over All the Powers of Darkness*" the following:

"You can dwell on the negative side of things and you will become what you dwell on. What you are thinking about and dwelling on is what you believe. What you believe is what you are talking about. And **eventually what you are believing and talking about is what you will become."**

He then went on to say:

"Many are defeated in life because they have a negative confession; they're always talking on the negative side of things, and that opens a door to the devil in their life... Invariably they go down to the level of their confession...

What a change would take place in your life if you stood your ground on the Word of God... **Then you would rise to the level of your confession...** take your rightful place in Christ and be able to possess what Christ has already wrought for you" *(Hagin, The Triumphant Church 167-168).*

What we give our minds to will inevitably control us. It is a simple fact: what we feed - will breed and what we starve – dies! If we feed our minds with junk then that's what we're going to process out of our minds *(and mouths)*

113

but if we feed on the Word of God continually then that is what we're going to process instead.

Remember also that the Holy Spirit is our *"Senior Partner"* and can only take-hold-together-with-us *according* to the Word of God. He will not agree with lies and profanity – as He is the HOLY Spirit. In fact He is the, ***"Spirit of God's Holiness."***

It stands to reason then, if we have more continuity watching television than reading our bibles – we can't expect to be transformed by something, we don't give ourselves enough to.

❖

Bibliography

- Billheimer, Paul E. <u>Destined to Overcome</u>. Copyright © 1982. Published by Bethany House Publishers. Printed in Michigan USA.

- Ekman, Ulf. <u>God, the State and the Individual</u>. Copyright © 1993. Published by Word of Life Publications. Printed in Uppsala, Sweden.

- Grubb, Norman. <u>Rees Howells: Intercessor</u>. Copyright © 2003. Published by The Lutterworth Press. Printed in Cambridge, United Kingdom.

- Hagin, Kenneth E. <u>The Interceding Christian</u>. Copyright © 1983. Published by Faith Library Publications. Printed in Tulsa, Oklahoma USA.

- Hagin, Kenneth E. <u>The Triumphant Church</u>. Copyright © 1995. Published by Faith Library Publications. Printed in Tulsa, Oklahoma USA.

- Hayford, Jack. <u>Prayer is Invading the Impossible</u>. Copyright © 2002. Published by Bridge-Logos Publishing. Printed in USA.

- Murray, Andrew. <u>The Ministry of Intercession</u>. Copyright © 1898. Published by James Nisbet & Co. Limited. Printed by Morrison and Gibb Limited Edinburgh.

- Strong, James. S.T.D., L.L.D. 1890. Strong's Exhaustive Concordance; Dictionaries of the Hebrew and Greek Words. e-Sword ® version 7.6.1 Copyright © 2000-2005. All Rights Reserved. Registered trade mark of Rick Meyers. Equipping Ministries Foundation. USA www.e-sword.net.

- Unless otherwise indicated, all scriptural quotations are from the HOLY BIBLE, NEW INTERNATIONAL VERSION ®. NIV ®. Copyright © 1973, 1978, 1984 by the International Bible Society. Used by permission of Zondervan Publishing House. All rights reserved.

- Scripture quotations marked AMP are taken from The Amplified Bible. Old Testament copyright © 1965, 1987 by Zondervan Corporation, Grand Rapids, Michigan. New Testament copyright © 1958, 1987 by The Lockman Foundation, La Habra, California. All rights reserved.

- Scripture references marked KJV are taken from the King James Version of the Bible.

- Scripture references marked MSG are taken from The Message. Copyright © 1993, 1994, 1995, 1996, 2000, 2001, 2002. Used by permission of NavPress Publishing Group.

- Scripture references marked NKJV are taken from the New King James Version. Copyright © 1982 by Thomas Nelson, 1982 by Thomas Nelson, Inc. Used by permission. All rights reserved.

- Scripture quotations marked NLT are taken from the Holy Bible, New Living Translation, copyright © 1996, 2004, 2007 by Tyndale House Foundation. Used by permission of Tyndale House Publishers, Inc., Carol Stream, Illinois 60188. All rights reserved.

- Scripture quotations marked TLB are taken from The Living Bible. Copyright © 1971 by Tyndale House Foundation. Used by permission of Tyndale House Publishers Inc., Carol Stream, Illinois 60188. All rights reserved.

❖

Ministry Profile

Doctor Alan Pateman, an apostle, is the President and Founder of **"Alan Pateman Ministries International"** (APMI), which was established in England back in 1987, a Christian-based *(parachurch)* non-profit and non-denominational outreach. This ministry is now focusing in two main areas: First **"Connecting for Excellence"** Apostolic Networking (CFE) and secondly, the teaching arm, **"LifeStyle International Christian University"** (LICU).

CFE is a multi-facetted missions organisation with the purpose of connecting leaders for divine opportunities and building lasting relationships, to touch the lives of leaders literally the world over. Apostle Dr Alan Pateman has to date ordained more than 500 ministers in over 50 NATIONS. In addition there are ministries, churches and schools who are in Association or Affiliation, looking to him for apostolic counsel and oversight.

Secondly LICU, which was founded in 2007, is a study program to help people discover their purpose and destiny. A global network of university campuses and correspondence students, demonstrating the Supernatural Kingdom of God through Doctrinal, Apostolic and Prophetic Teaching. Dr Alan holds the position of President/CEO, Professor of Theology, Biblical Studies and Apostolic Ministry. LICU is exploding throughout Europe, Asia and Africa, enhancing the Body of Christ

Dr Alan has authored more than 35 books including numerous teaching materials and LICU university courses (30) along with hundreds of Truth for the Journey articles on kingdom lifestyle *(that are regularly distributed globally via the internet).*

He is recognised as an Apostle, Bishop, Leadership Mentor, University Educator, Motivational Speaker, Connector and Author, who has also been featured on national and international TV and radio networks throughout the years.

Currently Apostle Alan, his wife Dr Jennifer reside in Lucca *(Tuscany)* Italy and travel out from their Apostolic Company.

- Alan Pateman Ph.D., D.Min., D.D., M.A., B.Th.

Academic Background

Dr. Alan Pateman attended several colleges throughout his training *(including studying Theology at Roffey Place, Horsham, UK and a Member of Kerygma - with Rev. Colin Urquhart and Dr. Bob Gordon - 1985-1987)* before being awarded a Doctorate of Divinity *(2006)* in recognition of his lifetime achievements by the International College of Excellence, now "DanEl Christian College" *(President: Dr. Robb Thompson USA)* also "Life Christian University" *(Dr. Douglas Wingate USA)* where he also earned a Bachelor of Theology B.Th. *(2006)*, a Master of Arts in Theology M.A., a Doctor of Ministry in Theology D.Min., *(2007)* and Doctor of Philosophy in Theology Ph.D. *(2013)* from LICU.

❖

To Contact the Author

Please email:

Alan Pateman Ministries International

Email: apostledr@alanpateman.com
Web: www.AlanPatemanMinistries.com

Please include your prayer requests
and comments when you write.

❖

Other Books

Media, Spiritual Gateway

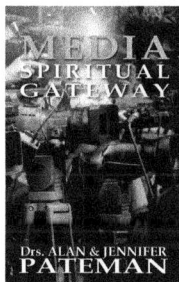

Let's face it; we live in the era of fake news! It's always existed, but never been quite so prominent. Today it's an all-out-war between fact and political fiction.

ISBN: 978-1-909132-54-2, Pages: 192,
Format: Paperback, Published: 2018
Also available in eBook format!

Millennial Myopia, From a Biblical Perspective

The standard for every generation is Jesus. However Millennial Myopia describes the trap of focusing everything on one particular generation or demographic cohort, at the exclusion and expense of all others. The Church cannot afford to make this mistake too.

ISBN: 978-1-909132-67-2, Pages: 216,
Format: Paperback, Published: 2017
Also available in eBook format!

Truth for the Journey Books

TONGUES, Our Supernatural Prayer Language

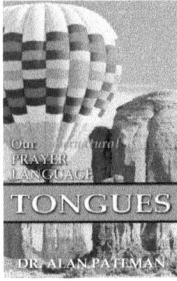

In writing to the church at Corinth, Paul encouraged them to continue the practice of speaking with other tongues in their worship of God and in their prayer lives as a means of spiritual edification. "He that speaketh in an unknown tongue edifies, charges, builds himself up like a battery."

ISBN: 978-1-909132-44-3, Pages: 144,
Format: Paperback, Published: 2016
Also available in eBook format!

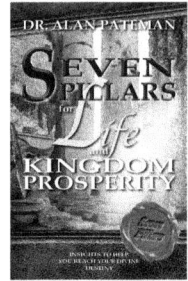

Seven Pillars for Life and Kingdom Prosperity

I submit these "Seven Pillars for Life and Kingdom Prosperity" to you, (Love, Prayer, Righteousness, Obedience, Connections, Management, Money). It's my desire that you walk in the triumphs that God has ordained for you.

ISBN: 978-1-909132-46-7, Pages: 220,
Format: Paperback, Published: 2016
Also available in eBook format!

Seduction & Control: Infiltrating Society & the Church

This book is a glance into the world of seduction and control, how they try to influence the Church through many powerful avenues such as the New Age, sexual education in our schools, basic entertainment; things that touch our everyday lives in order that we effectively and gradually become desensitised.

ISBN: 978-1-909132-00-9, Pages: 156
Format: Paperback, Published: 2015
Also available in eBook format!

Truth for the Journey Books

Kingdom Management for Anointed Prosperity

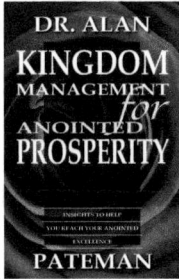

In his book, "Kingdom Management for Anointed Prosperity," Dr. Alan Pateman reveals how we can avoid living in continual crisis due to mismanagement. Life happens to all of us, but how we handle it matters most.

ISBN: 978-1-909132-34-4, Pages: 144, Format: Paperback, Published: 2015
Also available in eBook format!

Why War: A Biblical Approach to the Armour of God and Spiritual Warfare

Spiritual warfare means different things to different people, but from a biblical standpoint Ephesians 6:10-18 gives us the best biblical definition of spiritual warfare possible. We can also see how God has thoroughly equipped us for victory not just self defence!

ISBN: 978-1-909132-39-9, Pages: 180, Format: Paperback, Published: 2013
Also available in eBook format!

Forgiveness, The Key to Revival

Scripture is absolute when it comes to forgiveness. IF we forgive, THEN we are forgiven. It's that simple but no one said it was easy! Nonetheless, forgiveness can be likened to a spiritual key that unlocks spiritual doors and opportunities!

ISBN: 978-1-909132-41-2, Pages: 124, Format: Paperback, Published: 2013
Also available in eBook format!

Truth for the Journey Books

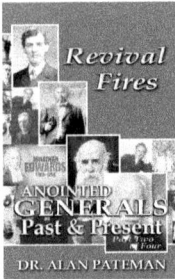

Revival Fires - Anointed Generals Past & Present (Part Two of Four)

Seasons might be changing but God's Word remains the same. The heart of the author is to help train, equip and be a blessing to those men and women who will be willing to fulfil their potential in ministry and be properly equipped for service.

ISBN: 978-1-909132-36-8, Pages: 142,
Format: Paperback, Published: 2012
Also available in eBook format!

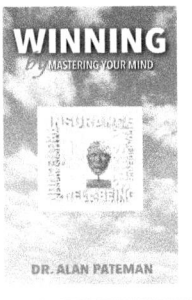

Prayer, Touching the Heart of God (Part Two)

Touching the Heart of God is the very essence of prayer. Whether we are petitioning God with very specific requests or consecrating ourselves before Him and rededicating our lives - whatever the case may be – the true essence of all praying is "Touching the Heart of God."

ISBN: 978-1-909132-12-2, Pages: 180,
Format: Paperback, Published: 2012
Also available in eBook format!

WINNING by Mastering your Mind

Someone once said, "Happiness begins between your ears and your mind is the drawing room for tomorrow's circumstances..." Remember, what happens in your mind will happen in time, and therefore one of our first priorities must be mind-management.

ISBN: 978-1-909132-40-5, Pages: 136,
Format: Paperback, Published: 2017
Also available in eBook format!

Truth for the Journey Books

Apostles: Can the Church Survive Without Them?

Before Jesus returns a significant increase of the anointing will be poured out on the Body of Christ, but can the Church handle such an anointing? *(Acts 5:5)* Billy Brim once said, "As much as the anointing is powerful to create, it is as powerfully destructive of evil." The fear of God will be restored with the apostolic and people will begin walking with such anointing, as we have never seen before!

ISBN: 978-1-909132-04-7, Pages: 164,
Format: Paperback, Published: 2012
Also available in eBook format!

Sexual Madness: In a Sexually Confused World

This book discusses the sensitive subject of political correctness in our world today and the growing fear of causing offence in the public arena. It also discusses the rise of homosexuality, pedophilia and all other forms of sexuality, as there are many. Including modern statistics on pornography.

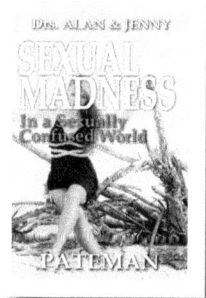

ISBN: 978-1-909132-02-3, Pages: 160,
Format: Paperback, Published: 2012
Also available in eBook format!

His Life is in the Blood

Blood is the trophy of every battle. The spilt blood of Jesus Christ is our trophy. It is our freedom from sin and bondage. Nothing can enter the blood-bought temples of the Holy Ghost! This book will encourage you to apply the blood of Jesus our Passover Lamb to your life, just as the children of Israel did in the Old Testament. Not merely talking or reading about it, but applying it.

ISBN: 978-1-909132-06-1, Pages: 152,
Format: Paperback, First Published: 2007
Also available in eBook format!

Dear Friends,

Have you considered becoming one of our international students? We are privileged to welcome you, from around the world, to "LifeStyle International Christian University" *(the teaching arm of Alan Pateman Ministries International).* **An English speaking university** dedicated to your success; to see you trained and equipped to fully succeed in your God given Destiny.

It is our passion to raise up the leaders of tomorrow, who will have influence in all realms of authority, including the Body of Christ. Men and women of strategy, wisdom and true godliness, who'll stand with stature and maturity in this hour.

It's undeniable that in today's world, recognised education has become indispensable, therefore it is our desire to offer well balanced and well structured courses. Those that have been written by gifted and talented ministers of God, who seek to be inspired by God's Holy Spirit.

Consequently we have put together a **flexible curriculum,** designed both for correspondence students and campuses, which is a strategy to reach the distant learner; whether provincial, national or international. In fact we have many correspondence students from around the world, including a growing number of successful campuses, in various countries.

This is a growing platform, where men and women of dignity and passion, can grow and be established in their God given endeavours. As God is the healer of the nations, we pray and believe that many of our alumni will go on to **become world changers** in their own right.

We are proud of each and every one of our LICU students.
It would be our pleasure if you would join them on this incredible journey!

Doctor Alan Pateman

Alan Pateman Prof. Ph.D., D.Min., D.D., M.A., B.Th.
PRESIDENT AND CEO
www.licuuniversity.com www.cfeapostolicnetwork.com
Email: info@licuuniversity.com   Mob: +39 366 329 1315

For more information visit our website/facebook or contact our office, using the details below:

Website: www.licuuniversity.com
Facebook: www.facebook.com/LICUMainCampus
Email: info@licuuniversity.com
Telephone: +39 366 329 1315

Partner
with us
TODAY!

We are looking to impact the world with the gospel, together we can do more! Join with us to equip the Body of Christ through our Apostolic Network, LICU university program, campuses, associated schools, missions, conferences, television programs, publication of articles and Truth for the Journey books.

You can become an APMI FOUNDATION PARTNER with a regular contribution of any amount, whether it is once a month or once a year.

- Receive monthly newsletters
- Connect with partners and leaders at our Connecting for Excellence international meetings
- Partners Dinners
- Personal availability for mentoring by Doctor Alan
- Enjoy complimentary books by Doctors Alan and Jennifer
- For those who GIVE EVERY MONTH £10, £15, £20, £30 or more will save money with special discounts on products, hotel rooms, conferences, and more

Partner With Us Today!
Call Italy: +39 366 3291315
Email: partners@alanpatemanministries.com
www.AlanPatemanMinistries.com

All Books Available

at

APMI PUBLICATIONS

Email: publications@alanpateman.com
*Also Available from Amazon.com
and other retail outlets.*

*If you purchased this book through Amazon.com
or other and enjoyed reading it, or perhaps one of
my other books, I would be grateful if you could
take a couple of minutes to write a Customer
Review, many thanks.*

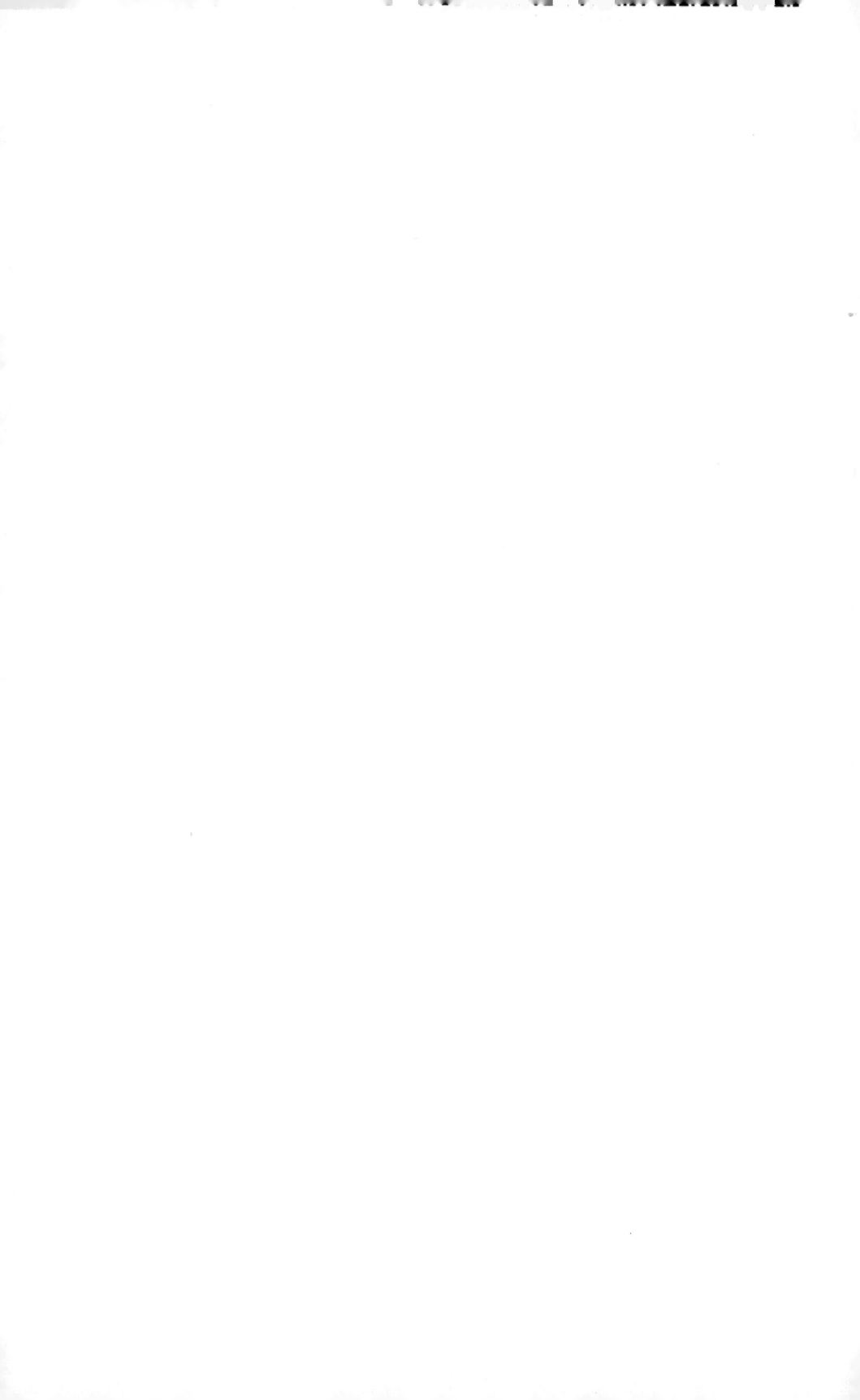

www.ingramcontent.com/pod-product-compliance
Lightning Source LLC
Chambersburg PA
CBHW071553040426
42452CB00008B/1151